OUT OF THE VORTEX

Edited by Rebecca Dias (Paper & Seed)

Published in the United States of America by Paper & Seed
PO Box 1245, Navasota, TX 77868 USA
www.paperandseed.com

Excerpt page ix from *The Art of Memoir* by Mary Karr. Copyright © 2015
by Mary Karr. Used by permission of HarperCollins Publishers.

Poem page 93 "if you can know one thing" from *Bending Serendipity* by
Fadi Y Sitto. Copyright © 2013 by Fadi Y Sitto. Used by permission of
Fadi Y Sitto. *www.fadipoetry.com*. Insta *@fadipoetryevents*.

Front cover author photo and photos pages 36, 52, 78, 84, 88, 114
and 118 printed by permission, courtesy of C. Beeler Brush.

Back cover author photo and author photo page 194 printed by
permission, courtesy of April Bennett.

All other photos are from the Whitehouse family photo collection and
printed by permission, courtesy of the Whitehouse family.

Cover and graphic design by Rebecca Dias

Printed in the United States of America

ISBN 978-1-7332377-2-7 (pbk)
ISBN 978-1-7332377-4-1 (ebook)

Library of Congress Control Number: 2020924857

10 9 8 7 6 5 3 2 1

OUT OF THE VORTEX

A Memoir

For Jeannie –
grateful to know you
amy whitehouse

AMY WHITEHOUSE

Paper & Seed, Navasota, TX

For Benjamin, Rachel, Faith, and Katie
I love you

AUTHOR'S NOTE: Writing my memories down has helped me find a sense of clarity, even wholeness. My hope is that putting them together into an ordered sequence may inspire or comfort someone whose life is touched by addiction. In order to ensure privacy, I have changed a few names. The stories are accurate to the best of my recollection.

"For the more haunted among us, only looking back at the past can permit it finally to become past."
—MARY KARR, THE ART OF MEMOIR

VORTEX: A mass of fluid, especially of a liquid, having a whirling or circular motion tending to form a cavity or vacuum in the center of the circle, and to draw in towards the center *bodies subject to its action* [emphasis added]

Webster's 1913

My people drank. In our home, drinking was as much a natural part of the day as brushing our teeth. I didn't think much about it since my aunts, uncles, grandparents, and friends' parents all drank, too. But every now and then I'd visit a friend whose family didn't drink. Those homes were . . . different. Cleaner? Safer? I still remember the feeling of security I experienced in those "different" homes. There was a sense of peace and calm that was lacking in my own. It didn't feel like the other shoe was about to drop at any time. I was keen to return to those places as often and for as long as I could.

Still, our family seemed to be high-functioning. My dad was a respected and sought-after attorney. Mother, at one time, was president of the Women of the Church, for God's sake.

By the time I got to high school I was making good grades, competing in piano competitions around the state, singing in the school choir, taking Communion on Sundays, and partying. I followed the example set before me.

As I grew into adulthood, I began to recognize alcoholism in my parents, my siblings, our extended family members.

But not in me.

PART 1

My Ordinary Life

Mother, Amy & Dad

1 · *Safe*

Soundtrack: Stevie Wonder, "Don't You Worry 'Bout a Thing," 1973

I squinted against the dazzling Florida sun. "I don't wanna go," I whined.

Daddy had just scooped me up from the beach where Mother and I were making sandcastles. He wanted to take me into the water. I was content to dig in the sand, hoping to reach China. Mother said if I dug deep enough, I would. I imagined a child in China digging too, our fingers eventually touching. Besides, I was terrified of the waves.

"C'mon, we'll just get our feet wet," Dad said.

"Noooo . . ."

"Don't worry, I got ya," Dad said as he hoisted me up on his bare shoulders. I loved it when I got to ride on his shoulders. He strode toward the water.

"But I don't wanna go."

"I know, sweetheart, we'll just go in a little way, and I won't let you fall."

"Don't go deep!"

He didn't even pretend to drop me; he held on to my legs draped over his chest. From where I was perched up high, it seemed like the water went on forever. I pictured China at the far end of it. Hearing Dad's feet splash as we entered that endless ocean, I looked down. The waves were rising higher on his legs and then whooshing away, coming back and whooshing away again and again. As we continued making our way out, I felt the spray reach my knees. I shivered at the sudden coldness, but the longer we were out there, the more I welcomed the water on my hot skin. Before I knew it, we were pretty deep. I was mesmerized by the in and out motion of the sea.

"Wanna get in the ocean now?" Dad asked.

"No . . ."

But he slowly lowered me from his shoulders so that my feet just touched the top of the water. The rhythm of the waves soothed my anxiety. Soon I was ducking my face into the dark green mystery and laughing. My dad and I were happy. All was right with the world.

Amy

My camphor tree

2 · My Tree

Soundtrack: James Taylor, "You've Got a
Friend," 1971

S itting on the curb with my feet planted in the street, I was
having a major pout.

The last time I'd stepped in the street, Mother had
switched me with a tender shoot from a bush. But this time no
one was at home, so no one could switch me. Everybody was
at the hospital for the baby. I didn't want a baby brother. Why
did we need a baby anyway?

I started getting ants in my pants, worrying that Daddy
and Mother might return any minute and see my feet touching
the road, so I climbed up into my tree and waited for the blue
Plymouth to chug down Fitch Street with my new brother,
Chanslor.

Some kids get a treehouse, some a playhouse, but I had a
tree. The camphor tree in front of our house was my hideout.
Easy to climb into, my tree had large, cozy branches that I
deemed rooms. One branch was the living room, one the bedroom, one the kitchen. I spent hours inspecting the shiny, waxy
leaves, pulling them apart to feel the sticky fluid inside.

My friend Oke often joined me in the tree to play house.
Though Daddy and Mother called Oke my "imaginary friend,"

she was good and true. I could count on Oke to be there when I needed her. Today I was too nervous to see Oke; the baby would be home soon.

Amy

Amy, Mother & Chanslor

3 · *Early One Morning*

Soundtrack: Hank Williams, "I'm So
Lonesome I Could Cry," 1949

Daddy parked the car on the street in front of the nursery school. As he was explaining that he had to get to work extra early, I looked out the window. It was darker than it normally was, and there was no one else around. It began to dawn on me that Daddy was leaving me at school early.

"The teacher's not here?" I asked.

"She'll be here soon," he said. "I'll walk you up to the classroom door, and you wait for her there."

I jumped out, slammed the car door shut, and ran to catch up to my dad. Not only was it darker than usual, it was cold, too.

"Stay right here, now, Little Amy," he said. "Bye-bye."

Daddy turned and walked back to his car. I watched as the car rumbled down the street.

Instead of staying in the shade where he'd left me, I walked over to the pavement where the sun shone and made a warm patch.

I concentrated on the goosebumps on my legs, willing them to go away, proving I was warming up.

How I wished Daddy hadn't needed to go to work early. I was four years old, shivering, and alone. A double dose of fear entered my body and settled in for the long haul.

Amy (top right) & nursery school friends

Dad & Amy

4 · *Social Hour*

"Children should be seen and not heard."
—English proverb, 15th century

I was sound asleep in my pink bedroom when the overhead light switched on. Chattering women entered my room clutching drinks that clinked with ice. Cigarette smoke wafted in as a few men followed a bit more boisterously behind them. I huddled down deeper into the bedclothes. My parents and their guests had decided it was music time. The old upright piano did not fit anywhere else in our small bungalow, so my bedroom served as the primary party venue at 3342 Fitch Street. I was five years old.

The year was 1958. All the men wore white shirts and black ties. The women's dresses sashayed in the tight quarters. I didn't mind the smells of the drinks and cigarettes, but the fact that no one spoke to me was unsettling.

These were our friends, they were always friendly to me. Maybe I was supposed to be asleep?

I stayed still and breathed small bits of air at a time, keeping the covers pulled up to my slitted eyes. I kept them closed halfway so I could pretend to be asleep yet see what was happening. Perhaps I was convincing.

As Mother settled on the piano bench, the party formed a

semicircle behind her. They leaned in to see the words on the sheet music and launched into "Bill Bailey, Won't You Please Come Home?"

> Won't you come home, Bill Bailey,
> Won't you come home?
> She moans the whole day lo-ong.
> I'll do the cookin' darling, I'll pay the rent
> I know I've done you wro-ong . . .

"Come sit next to me," Mother called to Uncle Billy as she played on. Dad's older brother quickly obliged, ashes falling onto the piano keys from the cigarette clenched between his teeth.

The group laughed and nudged one another, sharing innuendos I would come to understand soon enough.

> 'Member that rainy evening I threw you out?
> With nothin' but a fine tooth comb?
> I know I'm to blame; well ain't that a shame?
> Bill Bailey, won't you please come ho-o-o-me?

I knew the words by heart. It was a tune our family sang as often as we sang "What a Friend We Have in Jesus." I guess if I were in Bill Bailey's situation, a good friend would come in handy.

Mother shuffled through the sheet music for more songs, but mostly she played by ear. In my head I sang along with the grown-ups.

Dad was quick to notice a near-empty glass.

"Ruth, let me get you a refill."

"Oh, no, Jack, I have to be getting home."

"Well, you have to have one for the road."

"Make it a weak one, Jack."

Dad smirked. That was just the kind of request that inspired him to make it a strong one.

The party continued for a few more songs.

Eventually the sing-along came to a close, and the group trickled out of my room. Someone flicked off the light and closed the door. The shadows calmed my racing heart.

Amy & Taffy

5 · Bedtime Story

Soundtrack: "Rock-A-Bye, Baby," Nursery
Rhyme

"The whole house burned all the way to the ground?" I asked, even though I knew the story well. Routinely, my brother and I would go in to say goodnight to Mother before we went to bed. She'd be eating sliced bananas while propped up in bed with a magazine. Her blue box of Parliaments and glass of bourbon on the rocks would be close at hand.

"Yes, all the way to the ground. Nothing was left of our home," Mother answered, lighting up a cigarette and warming to the attention.

Chanslor just listened wide-eyed. Only two years old, he hadn't heard the story as often as I had.

"And did Dockie *really* carry the piano outside all by himself?" I asked.

Taking a long drag on her cigarette, Mother said, "Your granddaddy picked it up and carried it outside all by himself while the house was burning down. It was real hard for him, but he had some kind of supernatural strength."

Respectfully, we pondered the magnitude of this event. Dockie was like Superman to me. Not only had he saved the family piano, he had wrestled crocodiles in Africa! Every time we visited him in Virginia, he'd reach his fingers to the back of his mouth and pull out some special teeth.

"These here teeth, Little Amy, belonged to a nine-foot croc deep in the African jungle. I wrestled that bastard for six hours before I could wrangle his teeth out."

His magnificence held me spellbound.

"And tell about Aunt Tootie," I prompted, wanting Mother to keep going with the story. Chanslor needed to know the whole tale.

"Well, I kept trying to wake her up to get her out of the house, but she just didn't want to wake up," Mother said, tapping the ashes into the crystal dish by her bed.

"But she did finally wake up, and you all got out, right?" I asked, again for Chanslor's benefit.

"Yes, we all got out: MomMom, Dockie, Sonny, Ottsie, Tootie, and me. But there was nothing left except the piano. The house burned down because *someone* had been smoking in bed. That is why you never, ever, ever want to smoke in bed."

Here was the moral of the story: never smoke in bed. This was hard to absorb as Mother told the story from her bed while smoking. I didn't try to understand. It was merely one more knot of contradiction that defined our household. It did add to my repository of fear, however. I was old enough to understand there could very well be a fire in the middle of the night in *our* house. Years later I learned that mixed messages, such as this one, can contribute to mental illness.

After telling the story, Mother would lament her parents' nocturnal habits.

"Lord, I do hope your grandparents don't set their house on fire anytime soon. The way they drink and carry on . . . and always smoking in bed . . ." This was the usual benediction before we trundled off to our own beds for the night.

What with the nightly threat of fire, the explosive fights my parents sometimes had in the early morning hours, Mother's "nervous breakdowns," and the random invectives she spat at Dad, a palpable current of anxiety ran through our home. There was plenty for us kids to worry about.

Back row: Ottsie, Sonny & Tootie
Front row: MomMom, Mother & Dockie

6 · *First Drink*

Soundtrack: George Gershwin, "Summer-time," 1934

It was summertime and it was hot. The grown-ups sat in a circle within the shade of magnolia trees in my grandparents' backyard. We had driven to Virginia to visit Mother's family for a week. MomMom and Dockie lived in Fredericksburg, and all their children—Mother's siblings—had traveled from various parts of Eastern Virginia for this reunion. Uncle Sonny, Aunt Roxie, Uncle Ottsie, Aunt Tootie, and all their kids were there. Mother's name was Amy, but her family called her Babe. Even so, I was called Little Amy to distinguish me from Mother. It was 1959, and I was nearly six, just about to enter first grade.

The grown-ups rocked gently in the spring-based metal chairs. I was thrilled to be running around with my cousins. Chanslor was mostly on Mom's lap, too little to run with the big kids. We wandered in and out of the circle of chairs. The ladies were dressed in cotton shirtwaist dresses, the men in sport shirts and slacks. All the kids were barefooted and in shorts. The grown-ups were telling old family stories, laughing and wiping sweat from their foreheads as they sipped sweet tea or beer. In those days, kids fended for themselves. If we were thirsty, well, we knew where the hose was. It might have been warm water, but it was water.

I sidled up to Dad's chair, and he offered me a sip of his cold Budweiser.

Mother protested, "Jack, don't let her drink that," as she gestured with her cigarette toward the brown, long-necked bottle. "She's only six years old, for God's sake."

"Aw, it won't hurt her," Dad answered as I chugged as much of that cold liquid as I could with one swallow, knowing Mother's eyes were on me. It tasted heavenly.

Aunt Tootie had all us kids line up from tallest to shortest, me being the smallest, since Chanslor was napping at this point. She took a photograph, balancing her cigarette between her fingers while she pressed the shutter.

As the day darkened to dusk, we ran around catching "lightnin' bugs" in Mason jars. My cousin Becky and I slept that night on the screened-in porch, where it was cool. I was enthralled with Becky because she wore makeup and was a member of the Dr. Kildare fan club. As we say in the South, I was in tall cotton. And from that day on, Dad and I shared his beer.

Amy & cousin Chip

Amy, Chanslor, Dad & Taffy

7 · *The Year I Was Sick*

Soundtrack: Crosby, Stills and Nash,
"Helplessly Hoping," 1969

Held hostage in my pink bedroom for weeks on end, it didn't look like release would happen anytime soon. I'd had measles, then mumps, then a second strain of measles. Each time I started getting better, I was hit with something else. One morning I woke up itchy all over, even inside my mouth.

Mother came in my bedroom and said, "Dr. Palmer is on his way. Let's straighten up your bed and have you sitting up instead of lying down. He might give you another shot, so I want you to be brave and not cry." Having a well-mannered child was important to Mother.

Oh, no. Not another shot.

Normally when I was ailing, Mother took me to Dr. Palmer's office. From blinding Florida sunshine, we would enter the cool, dark building. The elevator operator would open the scissor gate to welcome us in. As the magical cage traveled up to floor 2, I'd stare at the metal plate on the wall and wonder who Otis was and how he got his name in the elevator.

Until summoned into the doctor's inner sanctum, Mother and I would sit in the waiting room with the receptionist.

If I was suspected to be contagious, we were required to sit out in the gray hallway, like some kind of interlopers. However, during first grade—my year of sickness—Dr. Palmer made regular visits to our house.

Mother coached me to "rise above," whatever that meant, and tried to convince me that if I did get a shot, it would make me feel better. Penicillin, the miracle drug of the '50s, was revered, as was Dr. Palmer. From my bedside window I watched the doctor's black DeSoto pull up and park at our curb, right beside my tree. His white head emerged then disappeared briefly as he reached into the back seat for the black bag that held the dreaded syringe.

"Hello, Little Amy, how are we feeling today?" Dr. Palmer asked, pulling the thermometer from his bag.

I hated having my temperature taken in my bottom; it was unseemly and uncomfortable.

"Now, we're almost finished," the kindly old man said.

He pulled the glass stick out and held it up in the air to squint at it. He shook his head a little and looked to Mother. "I'm afraid it's still high, and obviously now she has the chicken pox, even though she's just getting over the measles—again. How many weeks of school has Little Amy missed now?"

My heart sank. I had been "just getting over" measles when I got the mumps, and then had managed to catch another strain of measles after that. Now I had chicken pox. *I'll never get out of this bed.*

Mother balanced Chanslor on her hip and stood just outside my room so he wouldn't catch anything. She didn't answer Dr. Palmer; she probably didn't even know the answer.

"Can I still go to the circus Saturday with Aunt Florence and Uncle Bill?" I asked.

Mother looked at Dr. Palmer, and they both shook their heads. I turned away from them and slid down into the covers. I was trying not to cry just yet.

"One more thing, Little Amy," Dr. Palmer said, "but just you stay as you are and keep looking out the window. We'll make this shot as quick as we can."

Chanslor, Amy & Dad

8 · Scared

Soundtrack: John Fogerty, "Bad Moon
Rising," 1969

"What're they up to now, Jack? Can't even drive
the streets of our own town anymore," Mother said.

"Oh, don't worry, that rock throwing's not happening in
our neck of the woods," Daddy said.

"Maybe we should go home a different way, so we don't
have to drive near colored town."

"We'll be fine."

Florida was in the throes of Civil Rights protests, which
included people throwing rocks at cars in some city neighbor-
hoods. The news had been on the TV set at the bar of the club.

Dad was driving our family home from Sunday lunch at
the Seminole Club, as was our custom after church most Sundays. It was a private club, which meant members were white
and servers were black.

Even at seven years old, I knew something about my parents' attitude towards "colored town" was wrong.

This Sunday afternoon Dad had drunk more Scotch than
usual. His speech was starting to slur. The car lurched this way
and that, and my brother and I tumbled from one side of the

back seat to the other. Our car veered very close to the guard-rail of the highway. Afraid we were going to die, I was the most scared I'd been in all my seven years.

"Jack, you're about to go off the road!" Mother had her high-heeled right foot on the brake pedal on the passenger side. She used this imaginary brake regularly. Mother had a flair for the dramatic.

Chanslor and I giggled nervously in the back seat.

"I know what I'm doing," growled Dad. "And you kids be quiet back there, or I'm gonna pull over and make you."

I peered out the window to see if anyone was throwing rocks nearby. But mostly I was afraid Dad was going to crash the car.

We made it home all in one piece without a scratch.

Amy—Second grade

Sara

9 · *Sara*

Soundtrack: America, "Sister Golden Hair,"
1975

When I was seven years old, my baby sister was born. Sara entered the world weighing in at three pounds. She would always be petite, though her personality was sizable.

At age one, Sara broke out of her crib by tearing out the bars. She had jumped up and down on the mattress until the underpinnings gave out. The mattress stayed on the floor for months before Sara got a bed. In one family photo, she sat on the mattress between torn-out bars, her legs crossed and extended out onto the floor. Sucking her two middle fingers, she looked triumphant.

As a young child, Sara roamed the neighborhood and made friends with everybody, even people my parents didn't know. She was cute as a bug and had no fear. Mother and Dad joked about her wanderings. Fortunately, we had a *Leave It to Beaver* kind of neighborhood.

Bossy, loud, and insistent, there was no ignoring Sara. She had a keen love of animals, even insects. Once, I opened a drawer of a living-room side table to find a neat row of a dozen dead cockroaches. I knew instantly who had made the collection.

When Sara was six years old, our family took a drive to a nearby beach town. The country road wound through sawgrass under a canopy of live oaks in an undeveloped area outside the city limits. Without warning, Sara reached from the back seat over Dad's shoulder and grabbed the wheel, sending the car across the road into oncoming traffic.

"What the hell, Sara!" Dad shouted.

"You were about to hit an armadillo, Dad!" Sara shouted back.

We survived but were a bit shaken, except Sara, who was unfazed.

One Easter, our cousin Chip thought a cute little chick would be a great gift for Sara. The cute chick quickly turned into a rooster. Sara named him Pete. Our three dogs and Pete lived together amicably in the backyard. One Saturday morning, we noticed Pete limping.

"Dad," I said, "Pete's hurt and needs to go to the vet."

"I'm not taking a chicken to the vet," Dad declared.

Sara chimed in, "Please, Daddy, he'll suffer horribly if you don't. Pleeeease take him."

Dad took him. All three of us kids piled into the car with Pete. The rooster hopped from one lap to another on the frantic ride to the vet, scratching our thighs and arms.

Around this time, Sara brought home a stray dog. He was a cross between a basset hound and a beagle; we named him Gator. In Florida it was important whether you were a Gator, from University of Florida, or a Seminole, from Florida State. We were Gators all the way and now we had our own mascot. Pete the rooster would have to share living in the backyard with four dogs now.

My siblings and I had shaky relationships at best. But getting Pete to the vet was one time we all pulled together.

Mother

10 · *Summer Swim*

Soundtrack: The Kinks, "Sunny Afternoon,"
1966

I was very close to winning at Shark, the game we played every Wednesday in the neighbors' pool. Three kids were already out, tagged by Robbie, the shark. There were only two of us left, and I was determined to win. In order to better see which of us guppies would be targeted next, I wedged my left leg behind the metal ladder to boost myself above the water. Robbie was hurtling toward me from the other side of the pool. I wrenched my leg out from behind the ladder, quickly dove in away from Robbie, and felt a searing pain. When I climbed out of the pool and looked down, I was startled to see the skin was gone from three inches of my shin.

"Mother!" I cried.

She was sitting among the other mothers, chatting and sipping iced tea. She turned to look at me as I hobbled toward her.

"What have you done?"

"It hurts. Look at my leg."

"Oh, dear, you're going to need stitches," Mother said.

Vera, Mother's friend, piped up, "I'll watch Chanslor and Sara while you take her to the ER."

"Oh, I don't want to go to the ER," Mother said, looking at the other mothers for help.

"Audrey, you're a nurse, would you take her? I'm hopeless when it comes to blood." Audrey was already wrapping a towel around my leg as Mother spoke.

My mother doesn't want to take me to the hospital?

I could tell Audrey was taken aback, but she jumped to the rescue. "C'mon, Little Amy, let's get you to my car."

I held the towel tight against the wound and wobbled to the car. Mother stayed by the pool drinking her tea.

Sara & Amy

Amy

11 · *Turbulence in Fourth Grade*

Soundtrack: Steppenwolf, "Magic Carpet Ride," 1968

A lot was going on in the world in 1963. John F. Kennedy was assassinated; Beatlemania took hold in North America; George Wallace, in his inaugural address, proclaimed, "Segregation now, segregation tomorrow, segregation forever." *Lassie, My Favorite Martian,* and *The Virginian* were popular TV shows. The U.S. Postal Service initiated the ZIP code system. Hurricane Flora killed more than 5,000 in Haiti, Cuba, Trinidad and Tobago, and Grenada. The polio vaccine—given with a lump of sugar—was still relatively new.

But what I was concerned with was my fourth-grade class picture. Wanting to look my best, I had picked out my blouse with the Peter Pan collar and a plaid skirt. My seat was at the head of Row Two, front and center. I had a crush on my cousin's cousin Jerry who was also in the class. I imagined him gazing at my beatific smile once the photos were sent home.

My hopes were dashed. The night before the photograph was to be taken, Mother decided my bangs needed to be trimmed. Seeing her unsteady hold on the scissors, I knew this would not go well. I begged my drunken mother not to cut my hair. My resistance fueled her anger. Swaying and cursing, she insisted. I didn't know the word then, but I knew the feeling: I was powerless.

The resulting black-and-white fourth-grade class picture showed me with my hands clasped on my desk, a haunted look on my face. My blonde bangs were completely butchered: some parts were three inches long, other parts only an inch. Memories of her forceful, clumsy snipping still cause my heart to quicken and my stomach to ache.

1963 was also the year handsome Jerry had a horrible accident. It happened in our neighborhood near the drive-through liquor store my dad frequented and the one that would later serve an underage me. A car hit Jerry head-on. He was thrown from his bike and through the car's windshield. The impact caused his body to ricochet back through the broken glass, tearing his sweet face to pieces.

My parents tried to prepare me for Jerry's return to school. "Jerry is not going to look the same, Amy. You will be shocked, but try not to show it," Mother counseled me.

When he returned to school, a few weeks and a few surgeries later, Jerry was unrecognizable. His re-entry happened during lunch; his parents may have thought that would be a gentler time than early morning. My first sight of his mangled and scarred face horrified me. Since I wasn't supposed to show any shock, I tried to pass him in the cafeteria as if I hadn't seen him.

The spring of that year I had to get glasses. No one else in my class wore glasses, so I felt more self-conscious than ever. I pretended not to hear the whispers of "four-eyes" behind my back.

One day while sitting in the classroom, I suddenly lost control of my bladder. *I can stop this.* But the warm urine flowed down my legs and into my socks. It puddled under my desk. My face flamed. I was absolutely frantic, trying to come up with an explanation for this mortification. Only one thing was certain: my body had betrayed me.

I don't remember anyone ever speaking to me about the incident. No teacher soothed me, and no kids humiliated me with taunts and jeers. It was as if it were too terrible to even speak of. A nine-year-old psyche can handle only so much pain and confusion. This is my last memory of my tumultuous fourth grade year.

Later in life I came across the fourth-grade photograph. There I was with my botched bangs and hopeless expression. Jerry smiled innocently in the last row, pre-accident.

I thought again about what had happened to Jerry. He'd endured countless surgeries over those early years with minimal success. He never recovered emotionally and became a recluse. Sometimes Jerry would show up at a neighborhood party, but he'd always stay outside, under the huge oaks. Hanging out in the dark was probably as comfortable as he got. It seemed he spent the rest of his life lingering in the shadows. He made it to his fifties before committing suicide.

Enough. I lifted the top of the kitchen trash can and dropped the photo into the garbage. I closed the top of the can and let out one last sigh.

Dad

12 · *Crazy Making*

Soundtrack: John Mellencamp, "Authority Song," 1983

My parents drummed it into me to submit to authority and to never argue with my elders. Teachers and doctors and ministers were always 100-percent right. I listened to the Rolling Stones' albums and I had the trendy peace sign hanging on my bedroom wall, but I'd missed the suggestion to question authority.

When I did try to be assertive, I was squashed, and authority generally won.

One evening I went downstairs to the kitchen for a glass of water. There was Dad standing in his pajamas inside the pantry, chugging from a bottle of Dewar's. I'd seen such things before, but I'd never commented until that evening. I wanted him to know I saw him.

"Dad, why are you drinking out of the bottle?"

"I wasn't drinking out of the bottle. What are you talking about?"

What, indeed.

I'd seen what I'd seen.

Hadn't I?

Another night I woke up to Mother screeching.

"Go to Hell!"

"Aw, go to bed, it's late." Dad's voice sounded weary.

Oh, boy. My parents were at it again. It seemed like the middle of the night as I tossed in my bed hoping to regain oblivion. But I didn't get to sleep just yet.

Dad entered my room and sat on my bed. "Do you think your mom and I should get a divorce?"

"Gosh, Dad, I don't know." Inside though, I was screaming. *Yes! Please! It would have to be better than this, right? Why is my dad asking me what to do?*

Things got worse as the years crawled along. Crashing glass, profanities, hollering, scary silent pauses: all were par for the course on any given night. Sometimes Mother was the more intoxicated parent. Then Dad would have his turn. Uncertainty was the constant.

I retreated more deeply into my unfeeling fog and tried to get along as best I could.

Dad

Amy

13 · New School

Soundtrack: Gary Puckett & The Union Gap,
"Young Girl," 1968

"No, I won't go," I insisted, verging on tears. "I want to stay with my friends."

My parents had decided to move me from public school to a brand-new parochial school. At thirteen I was more scared than angry: it was an unknown. This was a brilliant move on my parents' part, and they didn't know the half of it.

My public school had students in eighth grade with names like "Bubbles" and "Bambi" who peroxided their hair, displayed well-developed bosoms, and carried switchblades. One day a message was passed to me to meet a certain girl behind the school at the end of the day. The implication was she wanted to fight me. This girl was jealous that a boy named Mike Batey showed interest in me. Mike was known as a hood, but I liked him. Think Danny in *Grease*. I scurried out the front door of the school that day, I couldn't get home fast enough.

Mike Batey did cause quite a stir. The gym teacher had noticed his attentions toward me and proclaimed loudly in front of gym class, "Amy Howell, you are going to the dogs."

Her manner indicated that this was an irrefutable fact, my destiny, if you will. Just one more pronouncement to add to my jumbled view of myself.

My school was the only one I knew, so despite its problems I wanted to stay there. But my parents ignored my pleadings to stay in Hoodsville, and I began ninth grade at the new school across town.

Most of the teachers at this newly opened school had been hired straight out of college, so they were only a few years older than the incoming students. My girlfriends and I made quick studies of the young male teachers, and decided they were more interesting than the students. We flirted brazenly, and the teachers behaved themselves, mostly.

There was one incident.

My friend Sharon and I arrived late to study hall. Immediately, the proctor sent us to the dean of girls. As soon as we reported to her, she marched us to the girls' locker room.

"All right, girls, I want you to undress and take a shower. This will be your punishment for being late to study hall," the young blonde dean ordered.

Sharon and I stared wide-eyed at each other, and reluctantly began undressing. Instinctively we turned from the Dean's lingering gaze at our fourteen-year-old bodies. Rinsing off and getting back in our clothes as quickly as possible, we were ready to get out of there.

"One more time, girls."

The second time seemed even more cruel. But we were programmed to obey authority, and so we complied. Again, Sharon and I exchanged glances, undressed, and repeated the sequence while being closely observed.

Walking back to study hall, Sharon and I briefly discussed

how weird that experience was but quickly moved on to other matters. We were embarrassed beyond words.

I never spoke of the shower experience until later in life when it shot into my head out of nowhere. I contacted one of my classmates and told her about this strange and disturbing memory.

She confirmed it right away. "Oh, that was Miss Smith. She did that to me one time, too."

PART 2

A Little Help from My Friends

Uncle Gene

14 · *Gift of a Lifetime*

Soundtrack: "Invention No. 6," J.S. Bach,
1723

I flew through the front door, sailing across the parquet floor to the stairway. It was my habit to take the steps two at a time up to my bedroom when I got home from school. I didn't make it to the top of the staircase before I paused and slowly backed down—one step at a time. Out of the corner of my eye I'd noticed something different as the living room blurred by, something huge and black.

There was a grand piano in my living room. I stared at it and tiptoed toward it. I was confused.

Mother entered the room, smiling. "What do you think?"

"What is this? Where'd it come from?"

"It's yours, honey. Uncle Gene got it for your birthday."

"But . . . *a grand piano?* Uncle Gene?" Tears sprang to my eyes as I caressed the matte black wood and slowly made my way around to the keyboard. I was afraid to touch the keys; the whole thing might disappear.

"Oh, my God. I can't believe it." I looked at Mother.

"I get to keep it?"

"You get to keep it. It's your birthday present from Uncle Gene," she repeated.

I'd forgotten it was my birthday. But, *this?* Who gives a present like this?

"Oh, my God," I whispered as I sat on the bench and tentatively started a Bach invention.

We had always had an old upright player piano with peeling white paint and a missing key here and there. I'd taken piano lessons since I was six. I'd never dreamed that we—I—would ever have something as extravagant as this.

Dad's younger brother was always a light in my life. His good-natured, generous spirit was a comfort in the increasing muddle of our home. He was also a Navy pilot, and whenever he came to town, it was cause for celebration. Dad would drive us out to the Naval air station to watch Uncle Gene's jet come in for a landing. He drank, too, but I never saw him drunk.

And now, on my fifteenth birthday, I had a real piano. I began to rise at 6 a.m. to practice for an hour before school. No one ever complained when I was playing, and I was free to lose myself in the music. I'd play a little more in the afternoon or evening. It was my refuge; I always felt better after making music.

My Uncle Gene was one of the friends who enriched my life.

Amy & her new piano

Paternal Grandmother Bess & Great Aunt Florence

15 · Crackers and a Pink Cadillac

Soundtrack: Bruce Springsteen, "Pink Cadillac," 1984

Dad always said we were Florida crackers. He'd had a hardscrabble youth, losing his mother to tuberculosis at age four and being shuttled around to various aunts and uncles across the country. During Dad's teen years, one caretaker began each day with an eye-opener of gin and orange juice. I eventually learned that all eleven of my grandmother's siblings drank to excess.

Dad taught me about the cultivation of roses and how to throw a football. When I was upset, he was the one to comfort me. But Dad tended to call us kids derogatory names like Big Butt and Bonehead. He must have picked up this habit in one of the various homes he lived in growing up. Teasing and criticizing became the ways we communicated in our home, too.

Mother never called us names, but neither did she kiss, hug, or speak words of love. Her indifference was worse than Dad's vulgarity. She also came from an alcoholic home, so my siblings and I had the cards stacked against us. Even genetically, it seemed we would not be able to avoid the taint of alcoholism in our own lives.

The miracle is that there were surrogate mothers in my life who poured love, comfort, and encouragement into me. They saved my life. The first of these was my great-aunt Florence, Dad's aunt.

Florence lived a few blocks from us. She might have felt a responsibility to me since my grandmother, her sister Bess, had died so young. At the time, all I knew was that she seemed to enjoy my company. Aunt Florence was the picture of decorum, her manners and language impeccable. She drove a pink Cadillac—a new one each year—and dressed fashionably, stylishly. She embodied refinement. Whereas Mother beseeched me to be ladylike, my aunt lived it. I remember quite fondly the first time she invited me over for afternoon tea. It was the year I started kindergarten.

Mother dropped me off at my aunt's house in the early afternoon. I was dressed in crinoline and patent leather shoes. This was a big deal for a little Florida cracker. Edna, Aunt Florence's live-in maid, greeted me at the door and ushered me inside with coos of affection. Her starched uniform was as immaculate as always, and her face sent moonbeams of love to my soul. I adored Edna, and the feeling was mutual.

"Oh, Miss Amy, don't you look pretty? C'mon in outta that sunshine. Oh, my, you are such a sight in those shiny shoes. Mmm, mmm, mmm," Edna crooned as she walked me inside.

Aunt Florence sat regally in the wingback chair, smiling at me as I reached the living room. Her graduated pearl necklace lay symmetrically upon her cashmere twinset, her slender legs were crossed demurely, and her silk heels matched her tweed skirt.

"Well, well, well, Little Amy, how do you do?" she said, smiling indulgently at me.

"Hey, Aunt Florence," I answered, picking my way across the lush carpet to the velvet love seat beside her chair. After jumping up on the cushion, I plumped my skirt out around me and let my feet dangle.

"You certainly look lovely today," Aunt Florence said as her long fingers flicked her cigarette toward the sterling ashtray. Elegance oozed out of her.

"Thank you," I said primly. Mother had coached me on that one.

Aunt Florence chatted with me like I was a grown-up. When Edna announced that tea was served, it was time to proceed to the dining table where two place settings awaited us. Dewy flowers from the garden had been cut and arranged in a crystal vase. Through pristine windows, rays of sun streamed across the table reflecting off the glistening flatware and silver trays of cookies. The hushed order was a contrast to my chaotic home.

"You ready, Miss Amy?" Edna asked. The bone china teacup was translucent and seemed fragile in my small hand. After I'd set the delicate cup back on its saucer, Edna carefully poured the hot tea.

"Would you like sugar, Little Amy?" Aunt Florence asked.

"Yes, ma'am, please." I helped myself to a heaping spoonful, proud that I remembered to use the scalloped sugar shell to pour the granules into my cup. I then stirred my tea with the proper teaspoon, the one at my place setting.

"Now, would you like cream or lemon?" My aunt gestured to Edna, who held the tray containing these added delights.

Oh, both looked good: the thinly sliced lemon on its china plate, the cream in its silver pitcher.

"I'll have both, please," I answered.

"You have to choose one or the other," Aunt Florence said.

"But I want both!" I insisted, being five and certain.

"Very well. Go on ahead," Aunt Florence said mildly.

I put lemon and cream in my beautiful tea, and promptly ruined it. My pride at stake, I knew I had to taste it. "That's horrible," I admitted.

My aunt nodded wisely but without reproach.

The lesson I learned from Aunt Florence was that I could make a mistake and not be ridiculed for it.

Florence died when I was ten. My parents didn't allow me to go to the funeral, saying I was too young. I hated not being able to say goodbye to Aunt Florence. Her photo remains in my bedroom, her pink Cadillac in my best memories.

Florence

Charles, Vera & Amy

16 · *Vera*

Soundtrack: Steve Winwood, "Higher Love,"
1967

In the South we always said, "yes, ma'am," "no, ma'am,"
"yes, sir," "no, sir." Even at four years old we were expected to pronounce "Missus" and use surnames. I properly
addressed Mother's friends, but when I met Vera and called
her "Mrs. Brown," she gently chided me and said, "You call
me Vera."

She was Mother's best friend and lived five houses down
from us. Her home was another enclave of refuge. At Vera's
house I was an esteemed individual, and I felt free to pop in
at a whim. If I could go back in time, I would visit Vera more
than I did, as a teenager, as an engaged young woman. When
our family moved away from the old neighborhood, our paths
didn't cross as naturally as before. Oblivious to growing apart
from her, I did not realize I needed her love and wisdom more
than ever.

When Vera's son and I were in third grade, we announced
to our mothers that we were ready to walk to school—by ourselves. Our mothers finally agreed, and the next morning we
set off for the mile-long walk to the elementary school.

Unbeknownst to Charles and me, our mothers trailed us in Vera's car like two TV detectives.

Years later when Mother was hospitalized for cirrhosis, Vera stepped up to the plate. I was fifteen, and my first date was coming up. An older boy had asked me to prom, and I needed a dress. Vera seemed happy to drive me around to stores in search of the right one. We found a quintessential '60s lace minidress with bell sleeves. I felt like a princess when I put that dress on.

The date was dreadful. The boy got drunk and threw up in the car on the way to the dance. I never shared the details with Vera or Dad; they would have been disappointed for me. But shopping with Vera fortified me in my mother's absence.

Another time, Dad asked her to help me find a bathing suit for the coming summer. We went to the most popular boutique in our neighborhood. Entering the cool store from the steamy Florida heat, I headed right to the bikinis. Vera took a stab at showing me the one-piece, skirted items. I nodded and went back to the bikinis. It didn't take me long to find the one.

"I don't know, darlin', it's awfully small. There's not much to it," Vera said as I pranced out of the fitting room to model *the one.*

"Oh, Vera, I just love it," I gushed. The fabric was a tiny brown gingham trimmed in white eyelet. It fit perfectly, and I knew it was the cutest suit in the store.

"Well, sweetheart . . ." Vera debated the wisdom of the bikini in question.

I continued to view my fifteen-year-old self in the full-length mirror, turning to judge the relative size of my derriere, hoping it wasn't as outsized as Dad claimed.

"All right, darlin', let's get it," she said, smiling.

Vera was always there for me. She had faith in me which added a measure of confidence I would need over my lifetime.

To this day we're best buddies. I live in Arizona, and she's still in Florida, so we only see each other once a year. But we call each other to discuss books and questions of faith and news of the neighborhood. And we always end our chats with words of love.

Frances & Amy

17 · *Frances*

Soundtrack: The Beatles, "All You Need is Love," 1967

Frances lived next door to us and was Mother's friend, but she was my friend, too. I could run sailing through her kitchen door as though it were my own house.

Once, at age seven, I appeared in Frances' kitchen in tears. She took me in her arms, grabbed a warm, damp washcloth, and dabbed my tears away. The gentle physical care was a new experience, revelatory even. Six decades later, a warm washcloth on my face continues to bring me a feeling of peace.

"Now you sit right down while I make us some pimento cheese sandwiches." Her voice soothed, the sun shone through her windows, the air sparkled with hope. Cold bottles of Coca-Cola and triangles of pimento cheese sandwiches appeared, and all was well. My soul felt safe and cared for.

Years later, when I was about to be married, Frances gave me a silver dollar. "Now, Little Amy, you call me if you should ever—ever—be unhappy. I'll come get you. You promise me, ya hear?"

Time passed in which I divorced, went to graduate school, remarried, lived in Europe, and started a family. I went to see Frances on visits back to Florida, though sometimes years passed between visits. When I brought Benjamin and Rachel, my two young children, along with me, Frances served iced tea and pimento cheese sandwiches at her dining table. During lunch, Rachel spilled her iced tea, and it immediately stained the beautiful linen tablecloth.

"Oh, that's fine," Frances said matter-of-factly. "I was going to soak this cloth in tea anyway to give it that antique look."

In the last years of her life, Frances' son Jay moved her to a nursing home. Before my annual trek to Florida, I called him to get the address of the care facility.

"Oh, Little Amy, she won't know you. She doesn't know who I am half the time, and I go over there every day."

That didn't deter me, but I entered the facility nervous and jittery. What was I supposed to do if Frances didn't know me?

As I turned the corner of a dim hallway, I saw a figure slumped over in a wheelchair at the other end. I started walking towards her and saw the woman raise her head. It was Frances peering down the hall. I saw a light come into her face, and her eyes began to focus.

"Don't you look beautiful, Little Amy," she said.

Amy & Frances

PART 3

Falling into the Vortex

Mother with pup

18 · *A New Disorder*

Soundtrack: George Harrison, "While My
Guitar Gently Weeps," 1968

I awoke to unearthly sounds coming from across the hall in
my parents' bedroom. I couldn't identify the alien noises,
but they struck fear deep within. Dad had left earlier to
take my brother and sister to school. I'd stayed home from
school, sick with a sore throat. It being just 8:30 a.m., Mother
would have still been sleeping. I felt compelled to investigate.
Fearfully I crossed the hall and opened the door. Mother's
yellowed eyes popped from her face, animal sounds emanat-
ing from deep within her. Though her eyes were pointed in
my direction, I could tell that she couldn't see me. Her body
thrashed about, jerking and convulsing on the bed. She didn't
respond to me frantically shrieking her name.

Fifteen and unprepared for an emergency, I ran to our
neighbor's house for help. She called an ambulance, which arrived quickly.

So began months of hospitalization for Mother. I heard
snippets regarding her condition: *her liver is three times its normal
size . . . she shouldn't have lived . . . an experimental surgery.* Dad didn't
enlighten us, and we didn't ask questions.

Our father continued his regular days at his law office, taking care of us as best he could. He'd always cooked breakfast for us—eggs, bacon, and grits every weekday morning. Adding dinner didn't seem to bother him, even if it meant an extra trip to the grocery store at the end of his workday. After dinner he would go visit Mother in the hospital.

Over the many weeks of Mother's hospitalization, family friends would occasionally bring us a meal. Sometimes a meal would be promised but never materialize.

"Who wants to go to the grocery store?" Dad shouted from downstairs when he got home from work.

"I do!" we all yelled from our respective bedrooms. After tumbling down the staircase we hurried out to Dad's car, still warm from his drive home.

"I want to sit in the front seat," Chanslor said for the hundredth time.

"Sorry," I said, not being sorry, "I got here first."

"Dad, can we get popsicles?" Sara asked. "And chips? And Coke?"

"I don't see why not," Dad said.

We tramped into the store, each determined to convince Dad to buy our favorite snacks.

"Amy, you get toilet paper and paper towels; Chanslor, bacon and bread; Sara, Coke and chips. I'll get eggs, milk, and hamburger meat."

As we began to disperse, I spotted Mrs. Jenkins down aisle 1.

"Dad," I hissed, "there's Mrs. Jenkins!" She had volunteered to bring our meal that evening, and we were excited and curious.

"Dad, go ask her what she's making for dinner tonight,"

we begged. Sara and Chanslor jumped up and down holding on to the sides of the shopping cart. I was too old to jump around in a grocery store, but I joined in the pleading.

"I can't do that; it wouldn't be polite. We'll just wait and see. It'll be something good," Dad said.

Too bad he didn't ask, because Mrs. Jenkins never showed. Dad made French toast.

I helped with dishes, vacuuming, and getting Sara dressed for school each morning. She was seven years old and anything but cooperative. Just out of pure orneriness she fought me when I tried to help her into her skirt and blouse.

Chanslor and Sara were both attending West Riverside Elementary, and I was a sophomore at Jacksonville Episcopal High School on the other side of the St. Johns River. Each morning I caught the bus for the hour-long ride across town.

That spring I was asked to display some of my artwork in the school library. I was proud to receive such recognition. My showpiece was a 16" x 20" oil painting of an African lion with a huge mane. Large cats were my passion in high school. Most of my paintings were displayed on the walls, but the lion had his own easel near the checkout desk. The exhibit ran for two months, but my parents never saw it. I told myself I understood why they didn't come, but I was still disappointed.

Mother was in intensive care for three weeks, and then in a private room for four weeks. She returned home thinner, weaker, and needier. She needed help getting out of a chair, help walking upstairs, help getting dressed. Before long, she relapsed and was back in the hospital.

When Mother returned home the second time, she committed to sobriety. Those were pleasant months. Mother had a great sense of humor and could be easy to get along with when she was sober. She laughed, played the piano, and told funny stories. It was a fleeting spot of sunshine in our family's life.

Amy & Chanslor—Atlantic Beach, with sandcastle

Amy

19 · *Unseen Parallels*

Soundtrack: The Bee Gees, "Stayin' Alive,"
1977

Once Mother had recovered sufficiently to attend church on Sundays, we resumed lunching at the Seminole Club. Dad would order Scotch on the rocks, while Mother ordered iced tea. But she wanted just a taste of Dad's drink.

After a few Sundays, she ordered her own drink, a whiskey sour. My stomach flipped. I knew there would be no turning back. Dad demurred, no doubt wanting to avoid any limits on his own drinking. Now it was I who wanted just a taste of Mother's drink. Did I hope she would drink less if I drank part of it? She allowed me to taste it. A heady concentrated lemonade of sorts, I loved it immediately. The family vortex began to swallow me up whole.

It wasn't long before I tried the drive-through at Monty's bar. I was alone and thirsty enough to take a chance. They served me a can of whiskey sour, no ID requested. I was sixteen and very pleased with myself.

Beer and mixed drinks were part and parcel of high school weekends. I went to every party I could, to escape the mounting tensions at home.

Mother began drinking again daily, and my parents grumbled about each other's drinking. Meanwhile in my world, I was using alcohol to allay my self-consciousness and insecurity. Alcoholism was working its insidious destruction on our family. The ironic parallels escaped my attention.

I learned it was cool to be able to hold your liquor. What sixteen-year-old doesn't have coolness as her primary goal in life? But mostly, drinking was comforting. It gave me a sense of confidence I didn't have when sober. I could be funny, calm, and self-assured whenever I was drinking.

Once I had my license, I occasionally drove myself to school. Having a screwdriver on my ride across town took the edge off any anxiety. I cradled the glass between my thighs, just like Dad always did with his beer when he was driving. I'd heard that vodka was odorless, so I counted on not getting caught.

Although I had close friends and made good grades, I never thought I measured up to the most popular kids. I was shy but covered it with bonhomie. A child of an alcoholic—in my case two alcoholics—doesn't know how dysfunction has affected her. She has been surviving and hiding instead of growing and developing.

Subconsciously, I knew I was deficient.

Mother & Amy

Amy

20 · *College Days*

Soundtrack: Jackson Browne, "Doctor My
Eyes," 1972

As the oldest, I was surely the luckiest of the three children. There were many pleasant times in our household as I grew up, but the unpleasant ones became more frequent as the years passed. My brother and sister had been born into a family that was already sick and growing sicker. I had a head start that neither Chanslor nor Sara had. After September 1971, I had to live with the deterioration only during school breaks.

My belief in my inadequacy increased when I went to college. I knew not a soul at Hollins College in Roanoke, Virginia. I was excited to begin freshman year, but even more, I was afraid. Afraid that I wasn't good enough to be friends with anyone. Afraid I would always be lonely. Afraid of not making good grades. I cried in the shower at night, but I didn't really know why. I was depressed and lost but couldn't identify the feelings with words. Nonetheless, I always looked forward to breaks and going home. I had a childlike notion that things would be better instead of the same or even worse.

It was home. It was what I knew. Despite their drinking habits, I held on to the concept that at any given time one of my parents would be stable—until one Christmas Eve when my illusion was shattered once and for all.

Both my parents were passed out drunk by 7 p.m. The stockings were hung but empty. *Santa won't find us,* I thought. I was home from college for the holidays and still counting on Santa to visit that night. I went in search of presents Mother or Dad may have purchased for Christmas. In Dad's drawers I waded through *Playboy* magazines and odd sexual cartoons he'd placed under t-shirts. I found some candy and gum that had not been opened. Next I crawled under hanging clothes on their closet floor. Behind dusty shoes and purses, I spied bags of gifts. After Chanslor and Sara had gone to bed, I placed the Christmas goodies under the tree in the living room. Gum and candies went in my brother's and sister's stockings. I stashed my stocking away so as not to bring attention to it being empty. On Christmas morning all went well. My parents each assumed the other had taken care of arranging the gifts. I didn't want thanks, just peace. After the holidays I flew back to college and returned to classes and partying.

Hollins was a women's college about an hour away from Washington and Lee University, a men's college in Lexington. Parties were held at the fraternity houses there every weekend. A bunch of us girls would pile into somebody's car and head over there most Saturday mornings and return to Hollins the next day. We'd sleep in frat houses wherever we could find a spot. Hungover every Sunday morning, I'd chastise myself for drinking too much and vow to stop. But by the next weekend it was the same scenario.

I began to have blackouts. I'd wake up on Sunday mornings with a groan. My mouth would be lined with a wool sock and my head would be breaking in half. I'd need aspirin and water immediately. Or even better, aspirin and a beer. The hair of the dog worked wonders.

One Easter Sunday I woke up with the familiar cotton mouth and headache. I looked around the unfamiliar room and wondered, *Whose room is this? Which frat house am I in? What happened last night?* My rising panic eased when I noticed my roommate snoring in the other twin bed.

"Courtney, wake up," I said as I nudged her side.

It was starting to come back to me. This was Carrington's room. And speak of the devil, Carrington himself strolled in just then, showered, shaved, and wearing a bright blue vest over his long-sleeved Oxford shirt. A Poindexter kinda guy.

"Happy Easter, girls!" Carrington shouted.

I heard church bells ring outside the window. I felt sick.

Oh, Lord, where is a cold beer?

Amy (center) & friends at May Fete

21 · Dilettante

"if you can know one thing
know you can love
if you can know two things
you know too much"
—Fadi Y Sitto

"Hello, Amy," a voice spoke from the living room. It was Mr. Sully, Mother's Rasputin. He was her close friend, home decorator, and caterer. Three years later, in June of 1975, he would orchestrate my wedding reception at our house.

I was home for spring break of my freshman year at college. Having slept in, I had just bounced downstairs in hopes of finding coffee in the kitchen.

Mr. Sully sat in the antique wingback chair he'd reupholstered as part of our living room redecorating project. Legs crossed, right hand airily holding his cigarette, he was dressed in his everyday orange jumpsuit.

"Oh, hey, Mr. Sully," I replied, gingerly stepping onto the new cream-colored Oriental rug. I knew we had to be careful with those new, expensive floor coverings.

Mother sat in the matching chair, sharing the crystal and sterling ashtray that sat on the heirloom table between them.

Directly across the room, Mother's portrait hung over the new couch. The painting was five feet high and displayed her in a romantic blue chiffon evening gown. Only a crown was missing.

"You've certainly disappointed your mother, Little Amy."

"Oh? How so?" I asked innocently.

"By refusing to be a debutante." He gazed at me over his exhaled smoke and continued, "You know, you're nothing but a dilettante."

During several seconds of silence, my mother watched her cigarette smoke curl in the air, avoiding my eyes and saying nothing.

"Ah, well, good to see you, Mr. Sully," I said as I backed out of the room to escape to the kitchen. I didn't know what that word meant, but I felt the barb attached to it. Mother's silence implied agreement, or worse, indifference.

Later I learned some synonyms for "dilettante": amateur, nonprofessional, unskilled. The definition implies one is pretending to be more of an expert than one is capable of being.

Coming out as a debutante was a long-standing Jacksonville tradition. It was considered a special honor to be invited into this exclusive coterie. I had received the invitation in the fall. My social-climbing mother had pounced on the opportunity. I, on the other hand, had no desire to participate. Why spend a boatload of money on parties to meet boys I'd grown up with? My parents and I had discussed this. I had been adamant that I was not going to be a debutante; I wanted to go on Hollins Abroad, a year studying in Paris. That program was why I had applied for early admission to Hollins in the first place. But just before spring break, I'd received a letter from Mother.

Dear Little Amy,

> *We are all so looking forward to you coming home
> for your break from school. Dad will pick you up at
> the airport as planned. Your room is all ready for you
> and the weather should be beautiful. Maybe we'll
> spend a day at the beach if it's warm enough. By the
> way, your father and I went ahead and accepted
> Jacksonville's gracious invitation for you to come out.
> Your friends are doing it, there will be lots of fun
> parties, and we'll pick out some cute dresses for you
> to wear. I'm quite sure you'll enjoy it.*
> *Love, Mother*

I was furious. My decision had been completely dismissed and replaced by Mother's pathway to higher social status. I prepared my case and presented it to my attorney father. The cost of being a debutante was roughly the same as spending a year in Paris. Did it not make sense to use that money on education and travel, rather than to be "introduced" to old friends? Dad agreed, and I won my case.

Mr. Sully was pleased with his clever but cutting play on words. Every time I've heard the "D" word—*dilettante*—I've cringed. The fear of being that kind of imposter has haunted me ever since. He considered himself a master in the realms of decorating, dining, and fashion. Too bad he didn't know love.

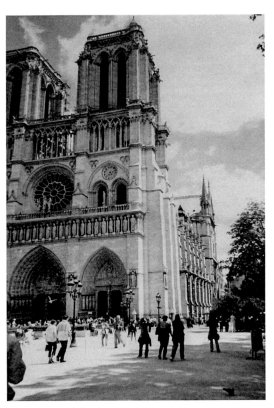

Notre Dame Cathedral, Paris

22 · *Life Abroad*

Soundtrack: Edith Piaf, "La Vie en Rose,"
1947

The flight from JFK to Orly took eight hours. We left New York one dark January night and arrived in Paris the following midday.

Our group of sixty young women were high on excitement, and the sparkly afternoon met that anticipation perfectly. We were routed to the French families with whom we would live for the coming year. Courtney was my roommate, just as she'd been since freshman year.

We met Madame, who escorted us to her car to drive us to our home for the year of 1973.

"I will speak to you in English only today," Madame said sternly. "Starting tomorrow we will speak *en français seulement.* And this will be the only time I will drive you in my car."

True to her word, after disembarking from her car in the basement with our suitcases, we never saw that car again. We were expected to learn the Métro system *tout de suite* and we did.

A stately, aristocratic home, the foyer opened into a living room that was elegant yet inviting. There was a formal dining room to the left of the entry, a tiny kitchen in the back, and bedrooms spaced throughout the apartment on Avenue Raymond Poincaré in the sixteenth arrondissement. Much later I would come to learn this was the upscale section of Paris, where the most affluent lived. Courtney and I had a privilege the other girls did not: we each were permitted a bath every other night. Some of the students only got one a week.

"Le dîner sera servi à sept quarante cinq heures chaque soir," Madame said, hoping we could at least interpret this simple statement. Foolishly, I had assumed that four years of French class had prepared me for a year in France. But I had no idea what she was saying. Our blank faces forced her to repeat in her uncertain English, "Dinner served at seven forty-five each evening."

Throughout dinner Madame spoke to us in French, still hoping we had some knowledge of the language, but she had to repeat most everything in English.

Madame was a *vicomtesse*, a woman of nobility, but needed the income from housing U.S. college students. Dinner was held formally and properly. Small glasses of water and even smaller empty wineglasses were arranged carefully at each place setting.

"Voulez-vous un peu de vin avec votre dîner?"

The fact that Madame was holding a decanter of table wine as she spoke was enough for me to answer, *"Oui, Madame, s'il vous plaît."*

She poured a paltry amount into the wineglass. Grudgingly, she refilled that tiny vessel only once per evening. It was clear that she disapproved of our having a second helping of wine at dinner. This was extremely disappointing.

We had four courses that night as we did every following evening. That first night our appetizer was a whole artichoke on a plate with a tiny bowl of melted butter. I didn't know what to do with it. Courtney was sophisticated enough to have done this before, so she gave me instructions from across the table. I learned how to peel an outer petal, dip it in the melted butter, and pull it through my front teeth to remove the soft flesh. Madame frowned slightly at the English we spoke, but I was grateful for the assistance. The next course, horsemeat, surprised me. But I was so hungry I ate every bit. *La salade* was served next, and finally cheeses and yogurt were presented for dessert. I fell into bed as soon as I could politely say, *"Bonne nuit."*

In the morning, as we'd been warned, Madame spoke to us only in French. She showed us how to make our instant coffee and where to find the baguette and jam. Coffee and bread were to be *le petit déjeuner* for the following year.

We were on our own for lunch, which was a problem for me. My parents didn't get the memo that I needed extra money for lunch every day. I had a small amount of spending money for the year, so I usually tried to make it through the day without eating. 7:45 p.m. could never come soon enough. Courtney and I were ravenous by that late hour. When Madame was not home, we searched the cabinets and found her stash of cookies. As the year went on, we helped ourselves to cookies before dinner as often as possible, guiltily giggling and miming Madame's potential arrival, catching us in the act. We laughed till our empty stomachs ached.

Occasionally a group of us students would venture out in the big city for dinner. Of course, the choices were vast and varied in the City of Light. I quickly found the restaurants that offered unlimited wine at communal dispensers. An endless supply of wine during dinner was my first qualification of a good restaurant. And I always got my money's worth.

Our classes were spread out over the whole of Paris. I signed up for remedial French right away, which was held at the Hollins Abroad office. My art class was near Sacré Coeur in the eighteenth district, but my film class was in the fifth district near Boulevard Saint-Michel.

I walked for hours every day to reach my classes. Once in a while I took the Métro, but that cost money. Sometimes I sneaked through the gate without paying. And *voila!* One day I was caught.

I had just ducked under the entry gate—ticketless of course—when a uniformed man grabbed my arm.

"Arretez! Arretez-vous, Mademoiselle!" He was pulling me toward a small glass-enclosed office where other uniformed men were smoking and looking angry.

"Venez avec moi," the first man said as he opened the door to the office.

"Que faites-vous?" a short, wizened old man asked.

"Où est votre billet?" another shouted.

It seemed they were all yelling at me at once. I was sure I would be arrested and thrown in jail. My whole body shook, and I could barely speak, much less translate and respond *en français*. After agitated discussion among themselves, they admonished me fiercely and released me. I took deep breaths as I walked the three miles back to Madame's house.

The thing about fear, about carrying it around in your soul your whole life, is that you don't handle it better as time goes on. You just add the weight of new fear to what's already there.

Understandably, the little money I did have was used at bars on the way home anytime I could eke out enough money for an aperitif.

It was cool to drink an aperitif, sure, but mostly, mostly, mostly . . . it numbed the fear for the moment.

Amy

23 · Entering Adulthood

Soundtrack: John Denver, "Sunshine on my
Shoulders," 1971

Coming back to the States after my year in Paris was a
culture shock, but I soon readjusted to American life.
Gradually, the billboards, the proliferation of McDonald's restaurants, and the disposable everything became normal
again.

Christmas at home was welcoming yet prickly. My parents'
alcoholism had taken a stronger hold; any previous restraint
they'd exercised was nearly gone. My brother lived in the garage apartment, where he was free to smoke weed and hide
from the world. My sister, Sara, had been kicked out of a couple of schools and was hanging on by a thread at the latest one.
I was twenty years old without a clue of where I was headed.

After New Year's, I traveled back to Hollins to finish my
junior year. There were a couple of cute boys at the nearby
men's school, but nothing developed beyond surface friendships. Still, I attended every party on our campus or theirs,
while somehow keeping up my grades. With no goals for the
future, I floated along, drinking daily now, not just on weekends.

The summer before senior year I went home as always. Mother and Dad had purchased a modest beach house for summers, renting it out to a teacher during the school year. I was happy to spend the summer at the beach, working at my dad's office a few days a week for pocket money. And then my life started to come into focus. It all happened rather fast.

I had a date scheduled with Greg, an old flame from high school. He was renting an apartment two blocks from my parents' beach house. The plan was to meet at his place and depart from there for our date. I walked the two blocks in my sundress and sandals, happily anticipating reuniting with this former quasi-boyfriend. We'd had a couple of dates in high school, but I always had been the more interested party.

When I rang the doorbell, it was Greg's roommate, Bryan, another high school classmate, who answered.

"Hey, Bryan, I'm here to meet Greg."

"Oh, sorry, Amy, Greg's not here. I think he went to dinner with his brother."

"Oh . . ." I was flustered and embarrassed to have been so easily forgotten.

"Why don't you come in from the heat and I'll fix you a drink?" Bryan said.

"Well, I guess I could do that," I said, entering the cool air of the bachelor pad.

"Have a seat on the sofa, and I'll be right back with that drink."

Bryan's curly brown hair was tinged with highlights from the sun, his tan was as dark as mine, and his broad smile seemed genuine. I'd never noticed how attractive he was. My disappointment began to fade along with all thoughts of Greg.

"This is a special Chablis I picked up last week," he said,

holding out the glistening goblet before sitting down rather close to me. We clinked glasses as he said, "Here's to Greg forgetting his beautiful date."

After he refilled my glass with the expensive wine, he insisted we have dinner right there at the apartment. "After all, you came here expecting a dinner date. The least I can do is whip up one for you. C'mon in the kitchen and keep me company."

And whip up he did. Bryan prepared a gourmet dinner of chicken parmesan, Caesar salad, and a fresh baguette. We finished a second bottle of wine before he walked me back to my parents' beach house.

Over the next few weeks, Bryan introduced me to fine French wines and high-end restaurants, as well as taught me the difference between Châteauneuf-du-Pape and Château Margaux. He was articulate and gorgeous, and I was smitten. We both loved reading in low chairs at the end of the day, dressing up for dinner out, having cocktails, and strolling the moonlit beach late into the night. I was starting to think it was meant to be.

Amy

24 · *Good Idea at the Time*

Soundtrack: Terry Jacks, "Seasons in the Sun," 1973

S ummer vacation ended, and Bryan and I returned to college to finish senior year. Our schools were in neighboring states, so we managed to spend nearly every weekend in one another's arms. Having never planned a career, I wished only to love and be loved, to belong to someone, to have a happy life. The subject of marriage came up that fall. I knew I would do it differently than my parents had. Our wedding date was set in June after graduation. Parties were held in honor of the upcoming marriage, gifts were delivered to our house, the church was reserved for the ceremony. But a few things gave me pause.

I learned that Bryan had been intimate with a few of the young women in our town. He'd mentioned going to a topless bar, which shocked me. His wedding gift to me had been chosen and paid for by his parents. A dissonance was percolating within me. But I swallowed my doubts and convinced myself it would all be wonderful. I was determined to have the storybook romance I'd always wished for.

A few days before the wedding, Mr. Sully (of the clever "dilettante" remark) and his wife threw a party for us.

Mrs. Sully, a compassionate soul, found me crying in a corner of her kitchen. "Darling, what's wrong?"

"I'm not sure I should get married," I blubbered.

"Oh, Amy, it's just normal pre-wedding nerves. It will be fine."

"I'm not sure," I said.

The wedding went as planned at the church I'd grown up in. The professional photographs showed a beautiful, smiling couple. But I had a gnawing feeling of disconnect.

Our wedding reception was exquisite, and held at my parents' home. The details had been decided by Mother and Mr. Sully with token questions directed at me about my preferences. After the receiving line was finished, Bryan spent most of the time joking around with his college pals. By default, I chatted with girlfriends. From the start we didn't operate as a couple.

Late into the dark, heavy night, we drove to a beach resort near Jacksonville for our honeymoon. The next day we began our new lives as a married couple. Bryan was starting graduate school, and I was going to support us. Securing a job as a secretary at a teaching hospital, my role as helpmate was one I happily embraced. Excited about this new beginning, I found an apartment for us, arranged for the utilities to be turned on, and bought a beautiful love seat for our first home. As our wedding present, my parents gave us the brass bed I'd always wanted, and I spent months finding the perfect desk for Bryan as my wedding present to him.

We moved in on a hot summer day, and got most of our belongings into our second-floor apartment by ourselves. Bryan picked up take-out pizza and a six-pack of Michelob. We ate our dinner on the floor since I had yet to find a dining table and chairs.

"Isn't this thrilling?" I asked between bites as I looked around our new living room. The carpet was fresh as was the paint on the walls. We were having our first meal in our first home, and I was joyful.

"Yeah," Bryan answered somewhat distractedly. "It's good. I've got to get my textbooks tomorrow."

"Well, here's to us." I held out my beer bottle to clink with his.

"Here's to us," Bryan repeated, finally looking me in the eyes and granting me his lopsided smile.

I felt optimistic.

Each month I paid the rent from my meager paycheck. I did the grocery shopping and made the meals and took care of the laundry and the housecleaning. If a friend of mine came over, we had to be quiet because Bryan was studying. If anyone had asked, I would have said I was happy, because this is what I so wanted to believe.

Bryan asked me to get contact lenses because he didn't like me in glasses. He also asked me to wear eye makeup. My job in the Radiation and Physics Department of the teaching hospital was boring and enervating. The scientists I worked for were brilliant men and women doing important work in advancing radiation treatment for cancer patients. I took dictation, typed up reports, and made purchase order requests in our basement office. It was pure tedium. It's no wonder I developed fantasies to keep my spirit alive. I had daydreams of Bryan dying and me being the beautiful, desirable widow who would find true love. Graduate school was everything to my husband, and I was hanging on because I didn't see any options. I ignored the voice inside that said I was dying until I no longer heard it.

"What's the matter?" Bryan asked when he walked into our

bedroom one night and saw me crying quietly.

"I really don't like my job," I sniffled.

"It's not forever. When I finish, it'll be your turn. You can go back to school, do whatever you want."

"Okay," I said. Wiping my eyes, I believed him and told myself I could do this for a while longer. But I was losing myself. I didn't know who I was or what I wanted anymore, if I ever did.

That weekend, instead of cleaning the apartment, I searched out my paints from the depths of the storage room. I hadn't painted since college. I propped up a canvas and painted my heart out. On the easel was the image of a dark, threatening sky above a house with a sagging roof. It was a dreary scene indeed, but it was something I'd created. Before it was even dry, I took it to Jacksonville and gave it to my dad. He immediately hung it in his law office directly across from his desk. Dad would see my painting all day every day because he was proud of me. My brain was foggy and didn't register the obvious symbolism of the artwork.

One evening a couple of years into our marriage—into Bryan's graduate studies—he suggested we go out for a drink. *How lovely*, I thought, *just the two of us*. We hadn't done anything like that in a long time because Bryan was always studying at the library. We drove to a neighborhood bar and ordered drinks.

"I have something to say to you," my husband said.

Something in his voice alerted my radar. I sat up a little straighter on the barstool.

"I want a divorce."

I couldn't have heard what I thought I'd heard.

"I don't love you," he continued. "I have never really loved you."

Our date had suddenly turned very sour. I'd had no inkling that Bryan was unhappy. He'd never brought up any issues or dissatisfactions. The dark barroom with the neon Budweiser sign started looking a little blurry. Stunned and speechless, I wept quiet tears on the bar.

I don't remember much more of that night. Before I could absorb what was happening, he was gone. He took our car, some silverware and plates, and left a stack of overdue bills on his wedding-present desk. Divorce papers arrived in the mail. I walked around like a zombie, staring into space, barely eating, numbing my loneliness with cheap wine.

I called home to tell my parents that my husband had left me. It turned out to be interesting timing.

My sister answered the phone.

"Hey, Sara, I need to talk to Dad."

"He's leaving."

"Well, tell him to call me when he gets back."

"I mean," Sara explained slowly, "he's leaving."

I paused to process that. "You mean he's moving out?"

"Exactly. He's moving out right now. He can't come to the phone. Bye."

Oh. Wow. No husband, no car, no parents, no plan.

Now being without a car, I had to ask my increasingly resentful girlfriend, Kelsey, for a ride to and from work every day. I started taking a lot of sick days. It was all just too hard. I began losing weight.

Upon returning home from a day I actually did work, I would lie down on my bed and my whole body would tremble. After an hour, I would get up and stare into the refrigerator, in hopes of finding something to eat.

This all happened right before Thanksgiving. With no car,

no offer from Mother or Dad to spend the holiday with me, no girlfriends, and $3 in my wallet, I was faced with a four-day vacation. Alone. That was one pitiful Thanksgiving. And, Mother had already told me not to come home for Christmas. That was her response to my offer to attend an A.A. meeting with her. I never felt so lonesome in my life.

Amy's painting

Amy

25 · Now What?

Soundtrack: Harry Nilson, "Everybody's Talkin," 1969

I was twenty-four years old and life had stopped. I hated my job and had no reason to get out of bed in the morning. My family was ninety minutes away, but no one called. Barely able to afford my rent and utilities, not to mention groceries, I didn't dare make a long-distance call.

One day I was at the grocery store to get a few things, when I caught the eye of a girlfriend. As I started to lift my hand to wave, she glanced at me and turned away. Another confirmation of my stark aloneness. The young women I had thought were my friends were simply wives of Bryan's grad school buddies. When he left, they did, too. I'd put all my eggs in one basket, and the basket had left town. I walked home from the grocery store carrying bags with cans of tuna, sandwich bread, and a jug of Gallo wine. My steps were heavy, my gait slow. I was in no hurry; there was nothing to go home to.

Kelsey remained my last link, and I depended on her, wanting to believe she really was my friend.

One day it didn't go so well. We had just pulled in to my apartment lot after work.

"Bye, Kelsey, thank you so much for the ride. I don't know

what I'd do without you," I said as I opened the passenger door to get out.

"You're going to have to find another way to get to work and get home. I can't keep driving you."

I felt I had been gut-punched with this abrupt reply to my thanks.

My voice shook as I tried to collect myself. "Oh, Kelsey, I don't know what to do. I didn't plan on Bryan leaving. This job was to support him, and now I need it to support me. I *have* to get to work."

"Well, Bryan was unhappy for a long time."

"How do you know that?" I was dumbfounded at this revelation.

"I probably shouldn't tell you, but he's been hanging out at our apartment every night for months. Talking about how he didn't want to be married anymore." Kelsey looked bored and restless as she spoke.

"Why didn't you tell me?" Shame filled me, but I wanted information.

"Oh, you know. He didn't want us to say anything."

"But . . . Kelsey, you're my friend." Sweat was running down my sternum, my mind was roiling.

"I've gotta go. Bye, Amy."

"Bye, Kelsey." I forced myself to sound neutral, swallowing the impulse to cry.

I climbed out of the car and closed the door. The late afternoon sun and sticky humidity made me instantly sweaty and nauseated. I dragged my ninety-five-pound frame up the stairs to our apartment. No, wait, it was *my* apartment, there was no "our" anymore. I avoided eye contact with my neighbors. *Where's Bryan?* I imagined them saying. *I haven't seen him around lately.* I didn't want to have to answer any questions.

Unlocking the door, I sat heavily on the love seat, now an ironically named piece of furniture, and stared vacantly at the ceiling. After a few minutes, I shuffled to bed, lay down on my side, and shook uncontrollably. The stress of the day, the reality of having been *left*, the knowledge I had failed completely—it all released through the shakes.

Isolated and discouraged, I lost more weight and often felt dizzy. Eggs and toast were breakfast and dinner. Lunch was too hard to plan, so I went without. After supper I'd watch TV and drink until I could fall asleep. The next day would be a repeat.

It has been said that alcohol is the drug of loneliness. Wine was always there for me as my companion—kind of like my friend Oke when I was five.

Unexpectedly, it was my dad who opened a door for me to start over.

Dad & Amy

26 · *Segue to New Life*

Soundtrack: The Beatles, "Drive My Car,"
1965

Dad drove me to the Honda dealership across town.
I was so excited—I'd never had a car of my own.
We got out of Dad's Lincoln Town Car and walked
toward the showroom. I was in awe, seduced by the brand-new
squeaky-clean cars with opened doors just inviting me to get
in the driver's seat.

"Ah, Mr. Howell." A smiling face approached us, a clean-
cut salesman Dad had obviously contacted ahead of our visit.
"And this must be Miss Amy." He extended his hand to me,
making meaningful eye contact. "Would you like to see our
new Honda Civic models?"

Would I ever.

"And what color are you thinking about, Miss Amy?"

Color? I get to choose a color? This was almost too good to be
true.

I ended up settling on a baby blue Honda Civic with a stick
shift and a tiny back seat. It was 1978 and air-conditioning was
not included. I didn't give a whit about that. I couldn't have
been happier had it been a Mercedes-Benz sports car.

We drove our cars back to Dad's place. Wanting to give my

father a hug good-bye, I jumped out of my car, my own brand-new car, and walked over to him.

"Dad, I just love it," I squealed. "Thank you so much."

"Well, sweetheart, you needed a car. Glad I could help."

Cranking up the radio and rolling down the windows, I drove off with a smile on my face and a lightness in my soul. It was time to put the pieces of my life back together.

Amy's Honda Civic

Amy & Mark

27 · Starting Over

Soundtrack: Johnny Nash, "I Can See Clearly Now," 1972

I determined that graduate school would be the next step. I took the LSAT and the GRE, applying to Florida law schools with vague interest. Although I was proud to be accepted by the two law schools I'd applied to, I had to ask myself, "Do I really want to study law for three years?" *Nope.*

"Get your MBA," someone said to me. "You'll make lots of money and be able to support yourself." Since I had no better ideas, I applied to the University of Florida MBA program and was accepted. I also received the student loans I requested.

Suddenly I had a full schedule of classes including accounting, computer science, microeconomics, and marketing. I didn't know what any of the professors were talking about. Reading the textbook assignments was akin to looking at hieroglyphics. I would calm myself at night with wine, beer, maybe weed if I had any. Then I'd try again the next day to understand the foreign language being thrown at me: paradigm shift, data driven, ROI, managing the optics, monetize, commoditize, trickle-down, diminishing returns, marginal utility. When I learned that calculus loomed ahead as a requirement, I knew I wasn't in the right place. I started looking for other options, and came upon the University's master's program in marriage and family therapy. I switched. Right away I was comfortable with the material, the classes, the professors, and the students. We spoke the same language.

While struggling through MBA classes, I'd met a young man named Mark Whitehouse. He invited me to play racquetball, and I accepted. He patiently taught me, and soon racquetball became a daily activity. We also began doing homework together for accounting and computer classes. Soon we graduated to pizza nights, movies, and my favorite—Saturdays at the beach. By the time I switched to the new master's program, Mark Whitehouse and I were a daily item.

On his ROTC days Mark was especially dashing in his Army uniform. He was different from anyone I'd ever known. I had grown up in a WASPish society-driven culture in Jacksonville. Mark had grown up in a military family, living in various countries around the world. He was attentive to me, and I was hungry for attention. Our drinking habits dovetailed, we enjoyed each other's company, and we talked for hours on end about anything and everything. As spring break approached, he invited me to his family's home downstate.

Mark's family was welcoming and hospitable, though I did hear "divorcée" whispered a couple of times. Alcohol flowed freely and that made me comfortable.

Soon it was time for Mark to meet my father. He had briefly met my mother already. We chose a weekend to travel up to Jacksonville.

"You're not nervous about meeting my dad, are you?" I asked while we drove north from Gainesville.

"Maybe a little," he replied as he jiggled his leg, shaking the tiny car, "but I'm sure it will be fine."

My parents had been divorced only a few months. Their breakup had been a bitter one. My siblings and I walked on eggshells now more than ever. If I spent ninety minutes at Mother's house, it was then okay to go to Dad's place across town for an hour. Mark and I pulled into the parking lot at Dad's apartment complex, quite modest accommodations compared to the refined and elegant home Mother occupied. My T-shirt stuck to my back as we stepped out of the car into the humid Jacksonville afternoon. It would be a relief to get inside the air-conditioned building.

As we approached the front door, angry voices announced something was happening inside. I knocked, then opened the door without waiting for an answer.

We stepped right into a fistfight.

Dad and his older brother, Billy, were yelling at each other and throwing punches. I didn't see any serious damage happening, mostly clumsy jabs from Uncle Billy.

Oh, boy, I groaned inwardly. My stomach churned the same old song it always played when I came home.

"Hey, Dad," I said.

"Amy! Hey! Billy, get yourself upstairs and sleep it off," Dad ordered his older brother.

"Hell, I don't need to sleep. I'm fine," Uncle Billy slurred. But he gave in and staggered upstairs, with Dad pushing him gently in the right direction.

"Dad, this is Mark. Mark, my dad, Jack."

The two men smiled at each other and shook hands.

"Want a beer, Mark?"

"Yes, sir. That would be great." My future husband had now been introduced to the Howell clan.

Florida country road

28 · Last Time

Soundtrack: Eagles, "Seven Bridges Road," 1980

As Mark and I grew closer, Dad began dating one of his clients, a petite divorcée named Judi. After asking my advice, "Should I marry her?" and receiving my routine answer "Gosh, Dad, I don't know," he decided to tie the knot.

Before Mark had to leave for Army officer training, we spent a weekend with Dad and his new wife. The four of us were eating lunch at the kitchen table when the topic of evening plans came up.

"Remember, I'm going out for drinks and darts with my brother tonight," Mark said.

It felt like a betrayal. He didn't realize the comfort his buffering presence was to me, and I didn't know how to communicate my need. "Oh," I said, "I thought we were all going to dinner at The River Club."

Judi broke in, "Amy, I want you and your dad to have a special time together. I'm staying home."

Oh, no. This is not good. My heart started pounding but I didn't speak up. What could I say—"I don't want to go to dinner alone with my father"?

I never would have felt this way before, when Dad was his old wonderful self. But more recently, he had become hidden, perpetually tense, and distracted. Alcoholism had more wholly claimed my dad, and I realized I didn't know how to be with him anymore.

Earlier that morning Dad had asked me to look up a number for him in his address book. He'd started this habit when I worked at his law office as a teenager. While he dialed the number and began his conversation, I flipped through his book mindlessly. Struck by the familiarity of a number under the designation "Z," my heart stopped when I realized it was my best friend's phone number.

"Dad," I said, as soon as he finished his call, "why do you have Marilyn's number in your book?"

"I don't know what you're talking about. I don't know any Marilyn," he said and walked out of the room.

I realized that Dad's lying had become pathological with the progression of his alcoholism. He lied about everything, including things that didn't need to be covered up. Honest, direct communication was gone. And now he and I had a special evening ahead.

I dressed in my silk chemise and heels, Mark headed out to spend the evening with his brother, and Judi settled on the couch in her pajamas.

Dad drove us downtown to The River Club, an exclusive and expensive dining club perched high above the St. Johns River. We parked and rode the elevator to the top floor of the Prudential building. We entered the club to the sound of live string music provided by a harpist. The lights were low, the diners spoke softly, the atmosphere was elegant. It was a serenely beautiful setting for the approaching disturbing memory.

Unable to wait till we had been seated, Dad ordered drinks on the way to the table. Nervous, jittery, sweating, Dad was the picture of inner turmoil. Our drinks arrived along with the heavy, cream-colored menus. We ordered our meals, whereupon Dad excused himself, purportedly to visit the men's room. I knew he'd made a beeline to the bar to scarf down a couple of shots.

Dinner was served, and Dad was still not back. I picked at my red snapper while his meal turned cold. The waiter replaced Dad's meal with a freshly made second plate when he returned to our table. Our conversation was stilted, halting. Dad had disappeared into a shell of anxiety and alcohol-laden stupor. I didn't have much of an appetite, and he barely touched his splendid meal. It was time to go.

We stood near the elevator waiting for it to take us down to ground level. Dad was swaying and leering at me. The scent of his Polo aftershave mixed with scotch and sweat was nauseating.

"If I were twenty years younger . . ." he slurred, eyeing me up and down.

His words sickened me more than anything he'd ever said or done before, and I couldn't wait to get away from him.

He insisted on driving home, and I didn't argue. I knew that any protests would trigger his drunken belligerence, which would make it all even worse. I endured the familiar swerving and erratic braking I'd known since early childhood. I never got in a car with him again. And in fact, that night at The River Club was my last time alone with Dad.

Dad & Amy

29 · Life with Father

Soundtrack: Eric Clapton, "My Father's Eyes," 1998

He hadn't always been like that.

Dad's favorite cousin used to tell me that my dad was the smartest of the bunch. I can hear Breezy's lovely North Carolina drawl now. "Jack was the chief. Even though he wasn't the oldest, he was in charge. When he was six, he said he was gonna be a lawyer."

And at twenty-one, Dad graduated from law school. He was a Florida Gator and a young whippersnapper, poised to take on the world. Over the years he developed a fine reputation as an attorney in Jacksonville. But also over the years, alcoholism tightened its grip on him.

When I was younger, Dad had been the reliable one, the caring one. Mother had been cool and unpredictable.

There was an accident when I was eleven. I was watching Sara, a fussy three-year-old, out in the backyard. I jumped up in the air with a cheer to distract her from her crying and came down—barefooted—on a rusty tin can hidden in the grass. Years before, Dad had scattered tin cans on the lawn to rid the yard of cinch bugs. Long forgotten, they'd become sharpened land mines. Dad wound towels tightly around my blood-gushing foot and bundled me up into the car. He sped to the ER and carried me into the hospital where they put us in an exam room.

"It hurts," I moaned while writhing on the examining table.

"I know, sweetheart, I know. We're gonna get you fixed up. Just keep looking into my eyes."

The doctor administered ten shots into the open wound. I kept my eyes on Dad and gripped his hand with all my might. The injections tore through me with a searing I had not known was possible. The stitches didn't hurt much, but a few hours later the pain was excruciating. Dad went to fill the prescription for the painkiller, and eventually I was asleep in my bed at home. I missed a couple of weeks of school.

A few years later I fell down the stairs at school and sprained my ankle. My stay-at-home mother didn't come get me; Dad did. And we took another trip to the ER.

As the years crawled by, our home life deteriorated. Glass crashed in the middle of the night as vitriol flew through the house. Dad disappeared most evenings to "take a walk," returning hours later to flee to the bathroom, turn the faucets on full blast, and retch. At the end I couldn't bear it, nor could I fix it. My parents were too far into the vortex of alcoholism, and it tore my heart into a thousand pieces.

Dad's final years were tragic, even though there was a certain relentless predictability to them. His marriage to my beautiful, young step-mother did not go well. There was Dad's suicide attempt and his admission into the psychiatric ward. He talked his way out of there the next day, and the whole suicide incident disappeared into thin air. No one talked about it. Later I was told that he hadn't tried to kill himself, it was just a big misunderstanding. I never got a straight answer from anybody about anything. I was left to work it out for myself.

My last few visits with him were hellish. Dad was skittery, nervous, restless. He couldn't hold my eyes for more than a few seconds before he excused himself to take a pull from a bottle, his prison. But in those moments, I caught the misery, the agony, the struggle that was my dad. His eyes were watery and red, his laugh sharp and forced. He never spoke to me about what was tearing him up, but his eyes betrayed his agitation. Always sweaty, he seemed about to implode at any minute.

Oh, Dad, what's happened to you? Where are you, because you're not here. I need you to come back. My dad's spirit was gone, and I knew it wouldn't be long before his body was gone, too.

My helplessness was as raw as a bleeding ulcer. Always connected more to Dad than to Mother, now I was tethered to him only through a symbiotic misery.

Having finished his officer training, Mark left for his Army posting in Germany, and I focused on finishing my master's and specialist's degrees in family counseling. After graduation, I put my belongings in storage, entrusted my beloved blue Honda to Mark's parents for safekeeping, and purchased a one-way ticket to Frankfurt, Germany.

Mark & Amy

30 · *Second Chance*

Soundtrack: Steve Winwood, "Back in the
High Life Again," 1986

After finishing my degree, I joined Mark in late September 1980. He was stationed in Bamberg, West Germany, a U.S. Army base occupied by American forces since the end of World War II. I met his fellow officers, his landlords, and his friends. We explored the beautiful town of Bamberg, dating back to the eleventh century, which had largely escaped major damage during World War II.

Being with Mark again after the year-long separation, I soon realized it was time to marry and officially begin life together. Mark had waited patiently for me to get over my cold feet. We planned the wedding around his parents' and brother's visit in December. Drawing up a guest list of friends from the battalion, we arranged a simple, small ceremony. We decorated the base chapel with luscious poinsettias and obtained a single rose for me to carry. Mark's commanding officer walked me down the aisle, and his lovely German wife was my sole attendant. Dave, Mark's only sibling, was the best man. After the reception we drove to a nearby village for a quick honeymoon. It was a cold, clear night. We were confident young lovers beginning life anew.

The fact that my family wasn't there was a relief. I could concentrate on beginning a marriage rather than managing alcoholic, divorced parents. It was as peaceful as it could be for me, and I was excited to marry my life partner. There was freedom in starting over in a foreign country.

German cathedral

Mark—Bamberg, Germany

31 · *Germany*

Soundtrack: Kenny Loggins, "Danny's Song,"
1971

Mark and I played like otters that first winter in Germany. Plowing down our snowy neighborhood hills on our new sled was exhilarating. We bought cross-country skis and swished for miles, always stopping at a brat haus for some local beer and brats. And there were so many new beers to try! Weizenbier, Bockbier, and Weissbier to start with. Small villages abounded in Germany, along with their local breweries. We wanted to try them all. If we were friendly with the owner, he'd invariably entreat us to sample his Apfelschnapps and Kirschschnaps. German wines were appealing as well: Riesling, Spätlese, and Eiswein. Oh, and the food was great also: Wiener Schnitzel, Spätzle, Sauerbraten, and Rouladen. Every village brat haus had its own garden, ensuring delectably fresh vegetables and salads.

We lived in a tiny village "on the economy," which meant a German apartment, not the Army base. We rented the second floor in a house with three levels. Our landlords occupied the small attic floor, and a couple of officers rented the bottom floor. I marveled when the village road was overrun by a flock of sheep, and all the cars would wait calmly for the fluffy animals to be herded to the next pasture. It was pastoral, like a picture in a storybook.

Mark was the aide-de-camp, the general's aide, while I counseled Army personnel and families at the Army's crisis center. At any given time, I would have suicidal, abusive, and/or multiple-personality clients. For the enlisted men living away from the United States, this life and its challenges were not something they were prepared for. I did my best but quickly realized my master's education was inadequate for this environment. I didn't have the life experience to be able to offer long-term help to those soldiers.

One weekend we went to Oktoberfest. Brats and more beer than I could imagine in one place. The women wore traditional Bavarian dress and hoisted the oversized steins with ease. Polka bands, dancing, and food vendors were everywhere. I did my part in drinking beer out of giant steins throughout the day. I don't remember the afternoon and evening or the trip back to our apartment.

Our landlords, Kurt and Elisabeth, were jovial and hospitable. Any conversation, no matter how passing, seemed to call for beers all around. On Christmas Eve they invited all the tenants up to their attic home to celebrate with champagne, beer, cookies, and candies. The Christmas tree was lit with real candles, which was breathtaking and frightening at the same time.

When I became pregnant, Kurt pressed a bottle of beer into my hand every time he saw me. "Good for baby! Good for you! It's *food,* you know," he promised.

I trusted his wisdom. After all, the Germans had been having babies longer than we Americans.

"And be sure to keep drinking beer after the delivery. It helps with the breast milk." I heard this advice many times, and

I was happy to comply.

Our application to live in base housing came through, and we decided to move so we could live within walking distance of our jobs, and close to the rest of the families in our battalion. We didn't have much notice, but quickly moved our meager belongings to our new apartment. At six months pregnant, I should not have helped move the heavy stuff.

Amy & Ben

32 · *Motherhood*

Soundtrack: Kenny Loggins, "All the Pretty
Little Ponies," 1994

"I think we should just drive over to Nurnberg and check it out," I said to Mark the afternoon of December 24, 1981.

"But the hospital is an hour away," Mark said. "We might not get back in time."

I knew the Army hospital was an hour away, but I figured I'd just have a quick checkup and we'd be back before our guests arrived. We had invited our Army friends to a Christmas Eve party in our apartment on the Bamberg base, and we had all the food prepared, even laid out on our dining room table. I was seven months pregnant and having contractions. I didn't think I was in labor; the contractions felt a lot like the Braxton-Hicks contractions I'd had the past few months. I just wanted to make sure that all was okay. Mark agreed, and we set off through the snow-laden Bavarian countryside in our tiny yellow Honda Civic.

Things did not go as I had planned. After I checked in at the Army hospital, the doctors transferred me to a German hospital. Once there, I was deposited in a dark hall. I heard the doctors discussing my situation, muttering about airlifting me to a special neonatal hospital. Nurses were passing out brown bottles of beer to patients. I had a faint hope of being given a bottle. The panic at my very center was beginning to blossom, and a beer would calm my nerves. The nurses did not offer me that solace.

The doctors decided to return me to the U.S. Army hospital. They put me in the maternity ward, where women were moaning and crying. The dim light and plaintive wails brought to mind images from 1948's *The Snake Pit*, the controversial movie about an insane asylum. A strong-looking nurse strapped me down on the bed. The level of fear within me rose even higher.

"Mrs. Whitehouse, you must not move from this position under any circumstance. Do not roll to one side or the other. Stay on your back just as you are. Here is your bedpan. Now hold out your arm while I attach the intravenous drugs your doctor ordered."

The medicine made me jumpy, like a heroin addict in need of a fix. Gazing up at the nearest window, there on the sixth floor, I imagined leaping through the glass in hopes of ending it all. For forty-eight hours I had to remain immobile on my back. Mark and I learned how to use a bedpan that Christmas Eve.

The doctors kept me for ten days, Christmas Eve through New Year's Day. I did get my own room once they'd stopped labor sufficiently to keep me on oral meds rather than the intravenous drip. It was a lonely ten days, and I was terrified for my baby's health and safe delivery. Mark made the trip from Bamberg to visit me nearly every night. I spent the days staring at the door of my room, teary and restless. Finally, I was discharged with instructions to stay in bed for the next four weeks.

A couple of months before all this my mother had called to say she would like to come be with me for the birth of her first grandchild. Her friends had offered to pay for her flights to and from Germany. This was a terrible idea. The thought of my mother visiting us, staying with us, doing who-knows-what with us was more than I could handle. I told her no. I would have loved a motherly woman to be with me, someone who would calm me, encourage me, instruct me on how to do all this. But that was not Mother.

"My mom is coming to help you for six weeks," Mark told me cheerfully.

What? Had I been consulted? Nope.

"Oh, and I'll be away on maneuvers for a couple of weeks during that time," he added. "It'll be great for you."

Noooo . . . this was getting worse all the time. I wanted someone, but not either of our mothers. Couldn't I pick someone else? Someone like Vera? But it had all been planned, and the trans-Atlantic flights were settled for my mother-in-law to come help. I swallowed any protests I had.

Due to complications, I had a Caesarean section delivery scheduled for January 22. Mark drove me to the Nurnberg hospital on January 21 to check me in. The following morning the anesthesiologist set up the intravenous epidural, reassuring me of its efficacy. Since I would not be under general anesthesia, Mark could stay with me and we would see the baby right away.

This did not go as planned either. Evidently the doctors could not see that the catheter administering the anesthetic had slipped out. Suddenly I was being cut open. Everything went red, then all black, then the doctors came back into focus. This sequence was repeated over and over within a matter of seconds.

I was never conscious long enough to speak, but I knew I wanted general anesthesia.

"She wants to see the baby first," I heard someone say.

I never said that! Put me out!

Mark was shooed out, the baby was shown to me, and soon I was blissfully unconscious. I woke up hours later to the most beautiful little boy who ever existed.

Somehow, Mark's mother had scheduled her flight to arrive four days after Benjamin's birth. Our precious son and I had just settled back into our third-floor walk-up apartment when my mother-in-law arrived. To say I was overwhelmed would be the understatement of the century. Benjamin was nursing every two hours around the clock. Mark's mom, Pat, would peer closely at my breast during feeding times, saying worriedly, "Do you think he's getting enough to eat?"

Of course I didn't know, but I was doing what the doctor had told me to do. I could have used some encouragement at that tender stage of mothering. I pushed through wordlessly.

When I did have a few minutes to close my eyes, Pat would invariably say, "Amy, shouldn't you be getting those thank-you notes done for the baby gifts you've been given?"

Wow. I just couldn't win, and it never got better. Though I had a master's degree in family counseling, I avoided any conflict and mostly kept my conversation to "thank you" for the meals Pat prepared. I was still a frightened little girl trying to be a mother ship.

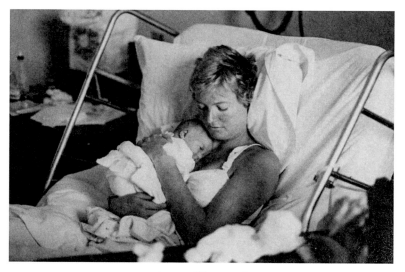

Amy—Hospital

PART 4

Climbing Out

Rachel, Amy & Ben

33 · Back to the States

Soundtrack: Barry McGuire, "Eve of Destruction," 1964

Once Mark had completed his Army commitment, we returned to the States and to civilian life. We landed in a podunk town in Southern Illinois where Mark found shift work at a plastics factory, and I tried to figure out how to be a mom. The best part of this three-year chapter was the birth of Rachel, a baby who sang in her crib and slept through the night. This latter quality was remarkable, as Benjamin chose not to sleep through the night until he was four years old. This caused minor but ongoing insanity in me, as sleep deprivation for four years is prone to do.

When Mark took a new job in Rochester, New York, life opened up a bit for me. Our neighbors became our friends, our church became our family. There was the symphony, the Lilac Festival, and apple-picking at nearby orchards. Our children started school, made friends, and took music lessons. Lessons led to concerts, more friendships, and summer music camps in Ithaca. We explored Niagara Falls, New York City, and Vermont. We built snowmen in the winter and taught the children how to swim in the summer. Benjamin and Rachel were the light and joy of our lives, and we enjoyed young family life. I volunteered at their schools, we dove into Suzuki music education as a family, we went to free concerts and Fourth of July parades.

Meanwhile, back in Florida, my parents continued to disintegrate. Our family of four drove down south once a year to visit Mark's family and mine, but these journeys were fraught with anxiety for me. Alcoholism's treachery made relationships more difficult than ever. I saw the addictive behaviors of my parents and siblings increasing, imprisoning them in their own irreversible, hopeless trajectories.

The downward spiral I witnessed caused me great distress. I began going to Al-Anon meetings to ease my anguish. Al-Anon meetings taught family members ways to cope with loved ones' addictions, primarily through teaching principles of detachment with love, relying on God, and sharing pain in safe groups.

I grappled with alcoholism being called a disease and still questioned why my parents made the choices they did. I felt obligated to visit them, but always came away from these trips drained and depressed.

As our little family began to grow and blossom, my family of origin was coming apart.

Ben & Rachel

Dad—JAG officer in Korea

34 · Phone Call #1

Soundtrack: Kris Kristofferson, "Sunday
Morning Coming Down," 1969

"Hey, Amy. I'm calling with bad news," Chanslor said. "Dad died."

My heart seized. All I could say was, "Noooo . . ." I repeated it over and over. When I could speak again, I asked my brother what had happened.

"Not sure, he was found on the floor of his condo."

Dad gone? No. This just can't be. I couldn't quite grasp it. I knew it was coming, but it didn't seem possible. Dad was 58.

I packed clothes and a cooler for the two-day drive to Jacksonville from Rochester. Mark and I were mostly silent in the front seat, and the kids mostly cooperated in the back seat. Having my family with me bolstered me for the upcoming ordeal.

I moved through those days as if walking underwater, with great effort and in a daze. Judi, Dad's wife, had arranged a visitation at the funeral home. Vera had welcomed Benjamin and Rachel to stay with her during this part of the funereal process. They played happily at her house, where I had found comfort all those years before.

I'd never been to a visitation and found it a most disturbing experience. The body in the coffin didn't look at all like my father. I wanted to remember him as he had been years ago when he was still acting like Dad: humorous, engaged, lively, and quick of mind. Instead, his face was made up and looked frightening to me.

Mark and I were in the parking lot of the funeral home that damp night when I heard someone calling my name. I could barely make out the figure in the soupy humidity, but I recognized the voice of Bruce Collins, an old family friend who'd consumed many a drink at our home while I was growing up.

Gasping a bit and reeking of alcohol, Bruce caught up with us. "Hey, I was just remembering your crazy dad," he said, reaching out to hug me.

"Bruce, this is my husband, Mark," I said, disengaging from his sweaty bear hug.

"Oh, hey, Mark, good to meet you," Bruce said, shaking Mark's hand.

"Yeah, your dad was somethin' else, wasn't he? I remember that time I was drivin' down Ortega Forest Drive and my headlights caught somethin' in the ditch," he went on. "It was your dad!" Bruce laughed gleefully as if it were the funniest story ever.

"Goodnight, Bruce, see ya," I muttered as I turned away and headed to our car.

Dad & Chanslor

Mother

35 · Phone Call #2

Soundtrack: The Rolling Stones, "19th
Nervous Breakdown," 1966

The last time I saw Mother, it was at her house. Mark,
the kids, and I had gone for our annual visit. We let
ourselves into her home, and I called for her. Slowly
she appeared in a doorway, bracing herself against the wall.
She looked somewhat green and apparitional. As she cautious-
ly made her way across the living room, she held on to a piece
of furniture with every step. She was not sober, but not fall-
ing-down drunk either. The living room stank of dog feces. It
was obvious that she and Chanslor had not gotten around to
cleaning up. The Oriental rugs—so carefully chosen years before with Mother's Rasputin—were ruined beyond repair. We
had iced tea, while Mother and Chanslor chain-smoked and
sipped beers.

A few months later, on Christmas Day, the phone rang
in the early afternoon at our house in Rochester. I answered
cheerfully, expecting a Christmas greeting.

"Hello? Merry Christmas!" I said.

It was Chanslor. "Hey, Amy."

"Well, hey, Chanslor, how's your Christmas?"

"Mom died," he stated matter-of-factly. "I found her on the floor a little while ago."

"Oh, my God."

I was underwater again, moving mechanically as I packed my bags and the children's clothes for another trip to Jacksonville. I pushed aside the feelings of pity, despair, and relief. It had been eighteen months since Dad died.

Mother's siblings arrived from Virginia before we made it to Florida. Mother had legally appointed Chanslor to be the executor, so he was in charge. At least nominally. On the day of the memorial, my brother was passed out drunk on the couch, and never made it to the church service. Sara flitted in and out of gatherings, beer and cigarette in hand. Having my aunt and uncle nearby provided some grounding for me.

I got through the memorial service feeling like we'd just been through this, which of course we had. I was numb and went through the motions as needed.

When I returned home to New York, I cried a lot. I tried to attend church with my family, but sometimes broke down upon entering the sanctuary. Once I spent the entire service outside weeping uncontrollably. I realized I was mourning what could have been.

Evaluating my experience as the daughter of two alcoholics, I asked myself, "Can I be a better mother to my children? Could I please not fail my kids as royally as my parents failed me?"

As my despair about my family and siblings increased, I began to attend Al-Anon more consistently. After visiting a few different groups, I found one I felt comfortable with. Ever silent at the meetings, I wanted to go unnoticed. I didn't know how to handle my life, what did I have to contribute?

The Twelve Step program encouraged members to find a sponsor who would help them through the process. After several weeks of attendance, I had decided who I wanted to be my sponsor. She was older and seemed well-equipped to walk through the Twelve Steps with a novitiate. I would have one-on-one, twenty-four-seven support, so I could really "work the program." I was excited to move forward. However, the woman declined to be my sponsor. I felt like I had been jilted at the altar. *What is wrong with me?* I felt embarrassed, sucker-punched, unworthy, but I kept going because Al-Anon was a secret healing place. And all I had to do was show up and say, "My name is Amy" and listen.

I began to learn some coping strategies. I was introduced to the concept of codependence. The people there talked of "detachment with love." Slowly, slowly, slowly I began to get it. I could do detachment with love. I could try to achieve the Twelve Steps. I latched on to the basics:

"Keep it simple."

"One day at a time."

"Fake it till you make it."

Someone always gave an introductory talk to get the ball rolling. At one particular meeting, my heart beat faster as I listened to the speaker explore the choice we had of forgiveness. Though feeling self-conscious and timid, I felt compelled to speak. "I think you have to forgive to get better," I said. It wasn't anything profound or new, but it's what I had to say.

As the meeting broke up a slim, Mary Tyler Moore-type woman approached me. "I really like what you said today. Hi, I'm Angie."

"Hi, Angie, I'm Amy. Thank you . . . what did I say, again?"

We laughed a little and exchanged phone numbers. Angie soon introduced me to Susie, and the three of us became fast friends. We saw each other at meetings but really got to know each other over lunches where we shared our stories. These were my encouragers and unofficial sponsors.

I began to heal.

Mother & Dad

Amy & Mark

36 · *Turning Point*

Soundtrack: The Byrds, "Turn, Turn, Turn," 1965

The spring air sparkled. We three Al-Anon friends, Susie, Angie, and I, met at a park to catch up. After another long Rochester winter, my spirit was light with the hope of summer. It was 1986, the year Reagan met with Gorbachev to end the Cold War. It was a time of promise.

Susie obviously had something to share and was excited about it. We'd barely gotten through morning greetings when she burst. "I'm going to A.A. now! I'm an alcoholic," she exulted.

What? *No, no, no.* Fear scratched at my insides. Susie wasn't an alcoholic. We weren't alcoholics. We were family members of alcoholics. What in the world was she talking about?

"What? What do you mean?" spilled out of my throat.

Smiling hugely, Susie replied, "I realized that I was an alcoholic also, not just my mother. So now I'm attending A.A. meetings." She looked like she'd just won the lottery.

I was stunned, confused. *No, no, no.* I didn't like this turn of events.

"Yes, girlfriends, I am an alcoholic, and now that I've realized it, everything's going to be great." Susie sipped a coffee while her gauzy white skirt fluttered with the breeze.

She looked so damned happy. I wanted to correct her, change her mind about this. And why was my stomach whirling around?

Later that fall, I accompanied my church friends, Barb and Helen, to a women's event. I was alone in the back seat, not really listening to the conversation taking place up front. I decided to tune in.

". . . so I resolved to get rid of all the alcoholic drinks in our house. And Tim is fine with it," Barb was saying.

Well that's a little extreme. I wouldn't go that far.

But something kept pestering me for attention, like an impatient toddler poking me in the stomach while my focus was elsewhere. No more alcohol in the house! I wouldn't do that. I couldn't do that. My wool sweater was starting to itch. "This is for you, Amy," I sensed someone saying.

Where is this voice coming from?

Who is talking?

I had believed in God since I was a child, and, despite all that had happened, I believed God was good. *Could this be God . . . speaking directly to me?*

I tried to focus on something—anything—else. But I couldn't drop it. Hours later, back at home, the thought came to me: "Alcohol has no place in your life, no place in your home."

The thought was crystal clear, and yet seemed distinctly from outside of myself. At least I never would have asked myself to do this.

No, this is about Barb, not me.

No, no, no. God or not, I argued back. I loved my wine before dinner. I needed those harmless glasses of wine. They were harmless, weren't they? If God were asking me to give them up, I could do that. Or maybe not. Couldn't or wouldn't. Which was it?

The wrestling continued. It was like the old Bible story of Jacob with the angel of God. The two of them fought all night. Jacob lost, and came away from the match with a lifetime limp. *What if I have only one glass of wine before dinner from now on? That would be okay, right?*

I was negotiating. Someone would leave this struggle limping, and it wouldn't be God.

Realizing this was a "no return" decision, my thoughts eddied around this conundrum. It was either no more drinking or challenging God's wisdom, which I knew more and more in myself to be true. What about the blackouts I'd had from drinking beginning in high school? What about the countless "Are you an alcoholic?" tests I'd taken in magazines and brochures? What about my consistent scores of 10 out of 10 for those tests: "Yes, you are an alcoholic. Here's where you can get help . . ."? What about that recent girls' getaway where I'd told myself to have not even one drink, yet the next morning I'd woken up on the hotel room floor next to my bed rather than in it, with the all-too-familiar raging headache and only vague memories of the previous evening? What about my children? Did I want them to grow up in a home like I did? That was a strong possibility if I continued to drink: I knew how denial worked. Could I stop drinking and show my kids life could be lived without alcohol? God's whisper-like voice had gotten my attention.

On November 30, 1986, I took my last drink.

*

Six months into sobriety. A couple of friends we hadn't seen since Germany came to visit for the weekend. I spotted a six-pack of Beck's beer on my kitchen table. Kryptonite. I was frantic.

"Mark, ask them to take the beer back to their car."

The beer disappeared, and somehow he smoothed the way for a comfortable weekend with our friends. I felt like a terrible host. But what else could I have done?

*

Five years into sobriety. Mark and I were sitting in an airport bar. Our flight was delayed, and we were killing time. The waitress asked for our orders.

"I'll have a vodka tonic, please."

Mark looked at me curiously.

"Oh, I mean I'll have a tonic water, please."

*

Eight years into sobriety. We were seated at a beautifully laid dinner table with our new Arizona friends. The host was pouring wine. I didn't want to stand out, I wanted to belong to this group. My heartbeat accelerated. I reached out and held my hand over my wineglass. The host passed me by. *They must think I'm a prude.* Mark also placed his hand over his glass. Solidarity was what I needed.

*

Nineteen years into sobriety. Away at a Christian women's retreat, my roommates-for-the-weekend and I went out for dinner. It had been a long day, lots of speakers, too much to think about. I was hungry, tired, and anxious.

A waitress passed our table with a tray full of tall, cold gorgeous glasses of beer, just inches from my shoulder.

My hand raised to grab a glass. *What was that? Amy, you almost reached out and took one of those glasses.* I scratched the top of my head and tried to look like I was studying the menu. That order wasn't even for our table. *Sheesh, get a grip! I know, I know, I don't know what came over me.*

*

Twenty-three years into sobriety. It was a hot Sunday afternoon in Phoenix. We'd been outside for hours at our daughter's soccer game. I was sweaty and wished I'd brought more water. Finally, it was time to go. We'd been invited to a friend's home, and I was looking forward to a lovely home-cooked dinner and some upbeat conversation. Soon I would be in an air-conditioned house. I walked through the front door and was greeted by our host. He held out a beautiful glass of white wine to me. The curves of the elegant wineglass were alluring. "Would you like a drink, Amy?"

Would I ever! I froze. My hand wanted very much to accept the proffered glass, glistening and sparkling with condensation. I couldn't speak. Glancing at Mark while making our friend wait for an answer, I stalled to muster fortitude.

"Um, I would love some water, please," I managed to respond.

Later I questioned myself: *Why did you behave so awkwardly? It's been over twenty years since you had a drink.*

I had no answer.

Sara

37 · Phone Call #3

Soundtrack: Dolly Parton, "I Will Always Love You," 1973

S ara and I never had a comfortable relationship. The closest we'd come was one Christmas, before my recovery, during a shopping trek to the mall. We shared cigarettes and beers, bellowing along with Dolly Parton singing "I Will Always Love You" over the car speakers. One had to enter the vortex to connect with anyone in my family, and this was one of those times of connection.

Expelled from three high schools, Sara eventually settled into a dancing school, where she was brilliant. Her feet bled from the toe shoes, but she kept dancing. Her long blonde hair brought to mind Rapunzel in her tower.

Once, she alluded to a brief affair with Mikhail Baryshnikov. Sara claimed to have conquered Misha, and she wanted me to know about it. I thought it vaguely crude for her to disclose such personal information. I realized late in life that she was always competing with me; I never recognized it while she was alive. Brimming with mischief and revelry, Sara was a wild child. She and our brother seemed to form a team against the world, our family, and me.

It's still unclear how I ultimately managed to escape the

vortex of alcoholism, whereas my siblings did not.

Sara called once from rehab when she was thirty-three.

"Amy, it's me."

"Hey, Sara. How's it going?"

"Not good at all. The money for my rehab is all gone, and I really want to stay another couple of weeks. I'm going to make it this time."

"Good for you, Sara."

"But I need money to be able to stay and get strong."

We wired the money.

The rehab supervisor called the next day. "Your sister broke out through her window last night and ran away."

Okay, then. Still breaking out, still going her own way.

During what would be our last conversation, Sara proclaimed that our dad was her savior. That proclamation told me she was doomed.

Years later another phone call came from Jacksonville. By this time our family was living in Scottsdale, Arizona.

"Hello?" I said.

"Hello, may I please speak to Amy Whitehouse?"

"This is she."

"Ms. Whitehouse, I'm calling from St. Vincent's Hospital in Jacksonville, Florida. Are you the sister of Sara Howell?"

"Yes, I am." My voice sounded small to me, as if I didn't want to proceed. I pictured St. Vincent's on Riverside Avenue, the same hospital where Sara was born.

"Ms. Whitehouse, Sara was admitted to St. Vincent's last night with an apparent overdose. Her body was beginning to shut down, so we started her on life support. However, we have to get your permission for further treatment. You are listed as next of kin."

My chest tensed and my mind raced. *What?* I hadn't been in touch with Sara for ten years, and now I had to make life and death decisions for her?

After nearly a week of daily calls from St. Vincent's, I realized I had to get to Jacksonville. I booked a flight for the next day, but she died before I got there. She was forty-one years old.

I arrived in Jacksonville to full responsibility. Sara was estranged from her three children and ex-husband, and was living on a boat with someone unknown to me. The hospital had warned me about a shadowy man who had brought Sara in. They had not allowed him to see her once she'd been admitted. All this left me to arrange for the cremation of her body and a memorial service at a church. The upside was that I finally met two of Sara's three children. She had never told them that they had an aunt.

The only information I had about Sara's final days had come by way of a phone call from Frances' son a couple of months earlier. My former neighbor told me about a surprise visit he'd received from Sara.

"I hadn't seen Sara in ages, Little Amy," Jay said in his Southern drawl. "It was nice to see her, but she didn't look well."

"I haven't seen her in years either, Jay."

"Well, it's the damnedest thing. The next morning, I couldn't find my wallet. I'd left it on my bedside table. Someone must've come in when I was asleep."

Jay was too kind to say it could only have been Sara. I didn't doubt it for a second. After all, it wouldn't have been the first time.

I still twitch when I hear a phone ring.

Amy

38 · Demons

Soundtrack: Judy Garland, "Somewhere Over the Rainbow," 1951

John refilled my shot glass with a bartender's precision. Our boisterous group filled the restaurant's biggest table. We were a congenial Bible study class, especially so when we were out on the town. John was our teacher and seemed to enjoy presiding over his devotees.

"Have another," he exclaimed with his crooked grin, "they're on the house." He caught my eye as he poured, and I wondered if he'd noticed I always had an empty glass awaiting the next shot.

Normally, of course, I wouldn't be imbibing. But this was one of those times it was permissible. I appreciated these respites from abstaining so diligently. It was allowed, right? My heartbeat kicked up a notch. My forehead felt sweaty. Wait a minute. What was I doing?

The room was dark, the blanket oppressive. My nightgown stuck to my body. I threw off the covers and sat up. I was hot and itchy all over. My mind reeled with anxiety and confusion.

It was only a dream. The one I'd been having over and over for a few years. In the dream I was in some kind of safe zone where I was allowed to drink whatever I wanted.

And every time I awoke from it, I had to breathe deeply and tell myself it wasn't real, merely a specter of my subconscious desire to drink. The process to calm down took five to ten minutes. I could always taste the drink whether it was a cold beer, a glass of white wine, a gimlet, or a bourbon on the rocks. I woke up with the taste in my mouth, so it was hard to believe it was only a dream.

A few days later my friend Ally and I were on the phone. "You could drink just a glass of wine now and then, surely?" she said. "I'm certain you'd be fine. Don't you think you could?"

"I don't know," I replied, knowing she just didn't get it. *Why does she keep bringing this up?* "I don't want to take the chance that I wouldn't stop." I tried once more to explain what it was like for me after half a lifetime of declining yummy drinks that I wanted with all my heart. It was futile. I often suspected my friends would be more comfortable with their drinking if I joined in the fun.

"So, Ally, how's your daughter doing in college?"

My question diverted our conversation to safer ground.

There were countless times when my own mind started the debate. *Amy, you know you have heart problems, anxiety, difficulty concentrating. You'd probably benefit from a small glass of wine, and it would be healthy for you.*

"Go away," I would say to the devils. I would grab a book, start a painting, check my email—anything to get my mind elsewhere. I wanted to shut down the perpetual inner questions: Could I? Should I? Why not?

Many years ago, I knew a young man who believed God wanted him to give up alcohol. He gave it up, and had a pleasant tie-it-with-a-bow story to share. "God just took away the desire to drink—completely. I haven't wanted a drink since the day He told me to stop. What a good God! He always provides, doesn't He?"

At the time I felt sure our good God would take away my desire, too. It's been 30 years, and alas, He has not.

Chanslor

39 · Chanslor

Soundtrack: Mark Knopfler and Emmylou
Harris, "All That Matters," 2006

I dreamed of my brother last night, my only brother, the one
I last saw some thirty years ago. If he were still alive, he
would be sixty-two now. The images I've had of Chanslor
these last few decades—living in parks and garages—cut me
like an old rusty knife. A deep, jagged cut straight down the
middle of my body.

There was a time when Chanslor was young, smart, wit-
ty, and handsome. There was a time when he graduated from
Marine training, when he stood erect and confident and was
self-possessed.

I learned of the last Chanslor sighting from a friend twenty
years ago.

"I saw your brother in line at the Salvation Army. I think
he was there to get dinner, maybe spend the night," my friend
said. "The next day I took a note to the facility and posted it on
the bulletin board. It said, 'Chanslor, your family wants you to
call them.' I left my number and sure hope he calls."

I've had fantasy scenarios in my mind including Chanslor
being married to a loving woman, living in a comfortable
home, having food in his pantry.

It wasn't my fault. I've told myself that, daily. But my soul forgets, and the pain lingers.

When I was nearly four years old, I sat on that curb in front of our house, pouting. I'd been the only child and had a selfish heart. I didn't want a baby brother.

When Chaslor was eight years old, he became very sick and had to be hospitalized. Mother spoke the words "spinal tap" in a way that frightened me. When he came home from the hospital he lay strangely still in his bed.

"Please go spend some time with your brother, Amy. He's alone all day in his bed. The least you could do is try to comfort him a little," Mother said.

Would that an angel from heaven had appeared to shake my hard heart out of my skinny chest and exchange it for a good heart. I didn't go in. I left him alone in that dark bedroom to get well on his own. If I had gone into the bedroom that day, would anything have changed for my brother's life? And yet, how could I have been to him what my Mother had not been for me?

There were some fun times to remember: playing Tarzan out back, swinging from the knotted rope Dad had hung from a tree limb; sneaking an unauthorized Coke from the refrigerator to share on a hot Florida afternoon; laughing at family nonsense during dinnertime. There were good times and awful times, but the unpredictability drove our constant anxiety. The stage was set for our intrinsic dependency on something to relieve the daily fear.

The ragged wound reopens whenever I contemplate what might have been.

Where are you, Chanslor? Are you hungry? Are you cold? Are you alone? Can you forgive me?

Recently I received one more phone call. Chanslor's high school friend had discovered that my brother had died, his body buried in a national cemetery.

Survivor's guilt is alive and well with me.

Ben, Faith, Rachel & Katie

Epilogue

During our children's adolescent years, Mark and I seized the opportunity to adopt a baby girl from South Korea. My commitment to sobriety, to abstaining from alcohol, was solid despite the near stumbles here and there. We felt like we had more than enough love in our family to raise another child.

Faith Elisabeth was a slender slip of an infant. Observant, quiet, and elegant even as a baby and toddler, she claimed our hearts the moment we laid eyes on her photo. Waiting several weeks for her to come home was excruciating. But once she was home, we all fell in love with Faith, and fawned over our new baby, taking turns holding and feeding and delighting.

Three years later we adopted Katie Hope from China. This little spitfire has been a force to be reckoned with, a strong presence. Katie's humorous nature brings us laughter, and her sensitive side reminds us to be compassionate. She grabs life by the horns and pulls us along with her.

Our family journey has had the full spectrum of experiences. God helped me make the right choice.

And now . . .

I want to raise a glass of champagne at a wedding instead of a glass of water. I want to dive into cocktails at parties and feel the tension of the day float away. I want to sit with my husband and enjoy gin and tonics before dinner as we did on our honeymoon a hundred years ago.

But daily I choose something larger.

I want to be coherent when my grandchildren run through my front door squealing and calling for me. I want my home to be clean, smell good, and be inviting for all. I want my kids to know they can count on me to be the same sassy, even-tempered mom they saw the last time they came over.

Sobriety is a remarkable gift and I'm glad I gave up on the drink. I know that I have done my part to break a chain of alcoholism that dates back generations. My kids and grandkids gather around our table for birthdays and holidays, and I marvel. The stories we tell and retell solidify our bonds, and our shared laughter makes family holidays nearly raucous. Conversation is wildly diverse, fast-paced, and humorous. No one is in a hurry to leave. No one is sneaking drinks in the bathroom or spilling cigarette ashes on my piano keys.

Even so, I'm not sure the drink has given up on me. Recently I had the task of transporting a jar of moonshine from Kentucky to Arizona for a friend. That jar sat on my desk for months before she and I could arrange to meet. The glowing amber winked at me daily. I thought endlessly about having a teaspoon of it and being done with the curiosity, confident I would be repulsed by the strong concoction.

Finally, my friend and I confirmed a date for lunch, and I would be able to hand over that beautiful temptation. Whew! We settled into a table at the Scottsdale resort my friend had chosen. Lunch was delectable, but the honey-colored liquid in the middle of the table kept demanding my attention. At last I could take no more.

"I just want to dip my finger in the white lightning to

see how it tastes. It's supposed to have an apple pie flavor," I said.

Surely that would reassure me that I no longer craved alcohol. It had been more than thirty years, after all. I was certain I was over it.

I unscrewed the lid of the Mason jar and touched the pad of my index finger to the surface of the glistening gold. Finger to mouth, I tasted it. It was divine. I wanted more.

"That's pretty good," I said, replacing the lid before pushing it across the table. "I hope you enjoy it greatly."

Hi, my name is Amy, and I am an alcoholic. This is my story of recovery.

To a Reader: If you recognize any signs of addiction in a loved one or in yourself, I urge you to connect with others who can support you. Hope, healing, and recovery are yours for the taking, but you must take the first step. Having attended Al-Anon meetings for years, I can attest to the strength and efficacy of 12-Step programs. For information on the fellowship of A.A. visit *www.aa.org*. If you are concerned about someone with an addiction problem, visit *www.al-anon.org*.

—*Amy*

Reader Discussion Guide

1. Some have questioned the purpose of exploring and writing about painful past experiences. What are your thoughts on the validity of such exploration? Why are so many memoirs being written?

2. Growing up in an alcoholic home can have lifelong consequences. Have you been touched by addiction? If so, how has it affected you?

3. How did growing up in the South influence the author's view of the world? What impact does local culture have on your life?

4. What were the positive aspects of the author's growing-up years?

5. How did the author's family-of-origin influence her development or lack of it?

6. The author noted specific help from friends. How do you think these relationships affected the author's worldview?

7. How do you as the reader understand the vortex metaphor in this memoir?

8. What do you consider was ultimately the author's reason for choosing sobriety? What were the difficulties she encountered with that decision?

9. Have you struggled with an addiction, and if so, how have you found strength and help to deal with it?

10. How was racism in the South depicted? Has it changed in the past 50 years? If so, how?

11. How might writing the story of your past affect your future?

12. Was there a soundtrack that stood out to you, and why?

Acknowledgements

First and foremost my thanks go to Rebecca Dias, my editor, publisher, and fellow artist. This book simply would not exist without her many hours/days/weeks/months of work. Her unflinching support, advocacy, and confidence helped me stay the course. Thanks to Fadi Y Sitto, poet and friend, for permission to reprint his beautiful poem "if you can know one thing" in my memoir.

Thanks to my writing teacher, Susan Pohlman. Her classes introduced me to the world of memoir writing, and her optimistic spirit spurred me on to write with both abandon and intention. Thanks to my draft readers, including Annie, Brynne, Christie, Rachel, Laura, Kate, Cheryl, Beeler, Julie, Shannon, Alice, Cynthia, Maria, and others, whose generous input helped my tentative scribbles to become well-developed chapters.

Thanks to Mark, Faith, and Katie, who have patiently endured sharing our dinner table with stacks of drafts, my huge thesaurus, coffee mugs, and general chaos the past few years, as I have pursued this dream.

And finally, thanks to my family of origin. I have to believe they loved me greatly and did the best they could for me.

AMY WHITEHOUSE grew up in Jacksonville, Florida, where family vacations at the beach inspired her love for the Atlantic Ocean. She received her M.A. degree in Family Therapy at the University of Florida. She currently lives in Scottsdale, Arizona, with her husband and two dogs, and escapes to Florida beaches each fall. Amy's twin passions are writing and painting. Her short stories have been published in *Canyon Voices* of Arizona State University, and in the literary journal *Gravel*. Her artwork can be viewed at *AmyWhitehousePaintings.com*.